Tall Ships

Tall Ships

The Golden Age of Sail

Philip McCutchan

Weidenfeld and Nicolson · London

Dedicated to the memory of my father,
Captain Donald Robert McCutchan, one of
the last master mariners to take all his
certificates of competency in sail and who had
acting command of a Cape Horner before
going into steam

Designed by Andrew Shoolbred for
George Weidenfeld and Nicolson Limited,
11 St John's Hill, London SW11

ISBN 0 297 77174 4

Filmset by Keyspools Limited, Golborne, Lancs
Printed and bound in Great Britain by
Morrison & Gibb Limited, Edinburgh

Contents

1

Before Tall Ships

opposite The *Vigilant*.

below The Vikings' early sailing ships boasted a single mast and were propelled by sail and oars.

I N the beginning ships were primitive things, small and functional, with no comforts – no deck even, just somewhere to sit and row, and be beaten with whips perhaps, or shot at with the stone-casting slings of ancient enemies. In the year 200 AD Roman merchantmen, carvel or clinker-built vessels navigated by two steering oars, one on each quarter, sailed the seas more or less unchallenged. Their two masts carried sail for propulsion – a single sail called the artemon on the foremast, which slanted out over the bow, and on the main a large square sail with two small topsails above. In the tenth century the Vikings sailed their double-ended craft, still with no deck as such; their warships were known as longships, and were propelled both by sail and by oars, while the merchantmen used sail alone. These craft were very manoeuvrable, the single mast, being stepped amidships, enabling them to sail even with the wind dead abeam.

During the thirteenth century the Nordic knarrs, and at the close of the Middle Ages the holks, were little more than developments and extensions of the longships; then came Columbus and the naos and caravels of Spain with their triangular lateen sails. From the start of the sixteenth century the carracks of Western Europe emerged, while from the middle of that century the kravels of Sweden sailed the sea; each type bringing gradually more sail area to send bigger and bigger hulls along until at the end of the sixteenth century the splendid galleons began to appear, with their great quarter-galleries around the sterns, richly decorated and gilded and now carrying topgallant sails on the two square-rigged masts, while the masts themselves were by this time split into lower, top and topgallant masts. From the middle of the next century we find the pinnace, again with more sail including spritsail topsails, until in 1620 the 'ship rig' as known to the clipper and windjammer sailormen began to make its entry, with all large ships throughout the world turning towards three masts with square sail on each, dispensing with the lateen-rigged fourth mast used by the stately galleons fussing along like overblown matrons.

The mid-eighteenth century saw the development of the frigates, which were basically merchantmen but were equipped with guns for self-defence. These vessels carried three masts, square-rigged on all. Square rig was now, in fact, firmly the in thing, and there was a natural progression from the frigates to the sailing merchantmen, the wooden clippers and then the iron, then the steel windjammers of the nineteenth century. There had been a great deal of development, but even so it is inevitably during the last one hundred and seventy years that the biggest changes of all have come about, as ships have turned from sail to steam produced first by coal, then by oil, to diesel, and then atomic propulsion. It is not entirely unlikely that lurking in some earth-bound sailor's heaven, some small port where still he can see and smell the ocean and feel the wind on his face, and have the company of sailormen, there is an old man who

A Spanish triple-decker at Naples;
painted by Abraham Willaerts, 1669.

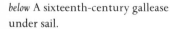

below A sixteenth-century gallease
under sail.

once experienced the thrill of 'snowy canvas set' – and now reads of the long underwater voyages of American and British nuclear-powered submarines.

Long gone are the 'forests of masts and yards' that once lined New York's East River, and the London River – as the square-rig sailors knew the Thames – below the warehouses now filled, where they stand at all, by the haunting ghosts of a glorious past. The aroma of spices, of baled wool, of tea that pervaded the great commercial centres of New York, Boston, the Chesapeake, San Francisco . . . of the Gulf of Finland, Nantes, the Elbe, Thames, Mersey, Clyde and the Bristol

Channel – those aromas were wafted with the clean scent of overseas trade into noses unsullied by petrol fumes. China, the Indies, West Africa, the great Southlands of Australia and New Zealand, the ports of South America, all these were linked to Europe and the Atlantic by the tall ships of the nineteenth century and by the men who sailed them, men from Britain and America, France, Italy, Germany, Scandinavia, Belgium, Holland, Portugal and Spain. Wooden ships and iron men: steam and the wooden men came later. The nineteenth century was, thankfully, the age of uncommon men who loved their way of life and accepted cheerfully – more or less – the dangers and discomforts, the long voyages, the loneliness and the absence for many months, even up to two years at a stretch, from their families.

The vessels that traded over the great sea distances of the world were of all sorts: the true ship – which had three or more masts, square-rigged on all – the barque, barquentine, brig and hermaphrodite brig, topsail schooner, brigantine, schooner, ketch, smack, lugger, cutter, yawl – these last three the smallest, the inshore handmaidens of the deep-sea carriers. They were for all purposes: mainly for carrying cargoes coastwise and to the seven seas but also and increasingly importantly as the years passed for the transport of passengers in varying degrees of comfort (or lack of it) from the horror of the steerage to the luxury of the first-class saloon. From sailing vessels too men fished off Iceland, the Newfoundland Banks – manning the Grand Banks Schooners which were some of the finest ever built – in the North Sea, the Lofotens, the Baltic, off the New England States; they chased after whales with harpoon guns, or they went to war. From Sweden, Holland and Portugal as well as from Britain they maintained contact with the great trading possessions in India by means of the beautiful ships known as the East Indiamen, which were merchantmen armed with cannon and run along the lines of naval discipline even to the extent that their masters were entitled to a thirteen-gun salute and a guard of honour upon their arrival in port. From Sweden, even the postman went to sea: the Swedish postal department owned mail vessels that in addition carried passengers and some cargo. The British Post Office also employed packets, armed against would-be pillagers of the Royal Mail, a contract existing between the General Post Office and the ship's master until 1823, after which time the British Admiralty took over and supplied ships for escort duty as required.

However, it was the deep-sea ship, barque and schooner that were customarily indicated by the term 'tall ship', though it is worth repeating that strictly the term 'ship' is in itself specific to a vessel with three or more masts and all with square sails: this was important to a mariner in the sailing days, for vessels were known according to their rig. Yet seamen often spoke of them in other and more colloquial and familiar ways, giving them the sobriquets that indicated their

overleaf 'Forests of masts and yards' lined the world's ports in the days of sail, as in the harbour at Leith.

The inevitable masts and yards, this time at Alameda, Oakland, California.

Full-rigged Ship

Barque   *Barquentine*

Brig   *Brigantine*

Schooner   *Ketch*

above Among the sailing vessels there was a hierarchy, a classification determined by number of masts and by quantity and type of sails.

origins: the limejuicers out of British ports and under British ownership, the blue-noses or Yankee hell-ships, noted for the brutality of the down-easter mates, the world's finest seamen perhaps, born for the particular purpose of fighting Californian grain around Cape Horn, but over-free with belaying-pins, knuckle-dusters and six-shooters. There were British hell-ships too, ships that made up their complements from drunken men put aboard by the boarding house masters, men who would not willingly have signed aboard the shanghaiing vessel. Punishments were always harsh, especially for erring apprentices: it was not unknown for a youth to be dispatched aloft to sit upon, or cling to as best he could, the foremast crosstrees even while on passage of the Horn, to be brought down hours later half frozen or even dead. There is a case on record where, in a ship outward bound around Cape Horn, an apprentice was shut in the hencoop for a whole passage of 150 days, never being allowed out even to wash away the droppings of his companion hens.

right A painting of the *Herefordshire*, one of the East Indiamen, so called because of their role in maintaining Britain's cargo contact with India.

It was a hard grind for the masters and crews who took the tall ships around the world and back again in return, in the case of an able seaman sailing out of a British port, for fifty shillings a month and meals of dandyfunk, burgoo, cracker hash, salt junk and slumgullion, with fresh water on a long passage being like gold-dust. A ship in the first half of the century would carry a crew of anything from twenty to forty men, and in a few cases many more, but in the later years the crews were much smaller, and probably even harder worked. Seamen had to provide their own clothing, including oilskins and seaboots, knives, eating equipment, and bedding – a mattress filled with straw and known as a donkey's breakfast. Few men alive today know just what the conditions could be like – the agony of lying out along an ice-coated yard off the pitch of the Horn to take in sail with frozen fingers from which the very nails had been torn, the only foothold being the swinging, swaying thinness of the footrope slung beneath the yard which could be 120 feet above a rolling, slanting deck; the racing seas shipped

To man the sailing ships crews put themselves at the mercy of the sea.

green over the bows as they plunged, to thunder aft along the waist while the hands on deck held fast to the lifelines and let the crashing sea flow over their heads. To dry out was virtually impossible: everything below would very likely be flooded, certainly the crew's quarters beneath the fo'c'sle would be awash with water surging from side to side below the narrow tiered bunks, dimly lit when lit at all by a swinging oil lamp, smoking and stinking. Yet they not only stuck it, they loved it: when at last a man went into steam, as for the sake of his career he had to by the end of the first decade of the twentieth century, he spoke of it, sadly, as 'leaving the sea'. A poet among them, Harry Kemp, wrote in *Cassell's Magazine* in the 1940s:

> I am eighty years old and somewhat
> But I give to God the praise
> That they made a sailor of me
> In the good old clipper days.
> Then men loved ships like women
> And going to sea was more
> Than signing on as a deckhand
> And scrubbing a cabin floor,
> Or chipping rust from iron
> And painting, and chipping again –
> In the days of clipper sailing
> The sea was the place of men.
> You could spy our great ships running
> White-clouded, tier on tier,
> You could hear their tramping thunder
> As they leaned-to racing near;
> And it was 'Heigh-ho and ho, my lad,'
> When we were outward bound,
> And we sang full many a chanty
> As we walked the capstan round.
> Aye, we sang full many a chanty
> As we drove through wind and wet,
> To the music of five oceans
> That rings in memory yet.
> Go, drive your dirty freighters
> That fill the sky with reek –
> But we – we took in skysails
> High as a mountain peak . . .

The sea seemed to greet the tall ships with a vengeance – pounding the decks, flooding the cabins and taking her toll of lives.

2

The Men Who Built and Sailed the Tall Ships

THE ships were beautiful, and the memory of their beauty helps to redress the balance of today's utilitarian drabness; but the men were men, and they must come first in any historical survey. The men who sailed the clippers, the masters and mates who drove them with their lee rails under, the men who raced them through the world's tempestuous seas, through the Sunda Strait for China tea and later down to the Leeuwin and the Great Australian Bight for wool, were supermen. They had to be, to survive. The weaklings were weeded out fast, rejected by the sea itself: there was no room for any but the best to remain at sea. The sea was a hard taskmaster, the hardest in the world, and a prover of men. During those long voyages across the world the ships were out of touch for weeks at a time – out of sight of land, away from all news of home, with no wireless or communication of any kind at all, and great wars could have been declared without their knowing. The responsibility borne by the masters and mates was immense, and the enforcing of discipline, so vital aboard a ship, a daunting problem in most cases, was best settled by the first mate's fist, for the crews were a mixed bag of fine seamen, drunks, shanghaied landsmen who had to be force-trained into sailormen, and criminals on the run. They could not be, and did not expect to be, kid-gloved.

The ships that became known as clippers – so called because they 'clipped over' waves rather than thrusting through them like the later windjammers – appear to have evolved from the early brigs and schooners built in Baltimore, the long, low, flush-decked vessels that dated back to the War of Independence, in which many of them had acted as privateers while others had been out-and-out pirates wearing the skull and crossbones, or slavers bringing black labour from West Africa. These vessels, of a type to bring out the best of seamanship qualities in their masters and mates, were exceptionally fast in quite light airs and in turning to windward, and their large beam, placed well forward, gave them a very fine run from the high bow, and plenty of sheer down to a low-set stern.

In 1832 a rich Baltimore merchant named Isaac McKim ordered from Kennard and Williamson, shipbuilders of Fell's Point in Baltimore, a ship that would embody the lines of these famous Baltimore vessels. The result was the *Ann McKim*, named after Isaac's wife. She was of 493 tons register, 143 feet in length with a beam of 31 feet and depth of 14 feet; and it could be said that she was the first of the clippers as they were to become known to subsequent generations. *Ann McKim* was a handsome little vessel, built regardless of expense. She had good dead-rise at her midship section, with long and easy convex lines, a low freeboard with her stem, stern-post and masts wonderfully raked. She was ship-rigged – that is to say, she had the standard three masts, all of them carrying square sail. She had frames of live oak, copper-fastened throughout, her stern was sheathed with specially imported red copper, her flush deck was fitted with hatch

opposite The self-sufficiency of the sailing ships demanded that the crew be competent at maintaining her. Aboard the *Beatrice*, the carpenter repairs a yard.

A nineteenth-century view of the harbour at Baltimore, birthplace of the clippers.

coamings of mahogany from Spain, her rails, companions and skylights being of the same wood; and she mounted twelve brass guns. Very fast, though not a big cargo-carrier, she spent her early years in the China trade, but in 1847 was sold at Valparaiso and passed under the Chilean flag.

Before the time of the *Ann McKim*, the noted American Black Ball Line had in 1815 pioneered the North Atlantic packet ships. *Amity, Pacific, James Monroe*, and later *New York, Eagle, James Cropper, William Thompson, Albion* and *Canada* were all flush-decked ships with comfortable cabins, even luxurious by the standards of the day, with steerage passengers below in the 'tween-decks. The hulls were black painted with boats and upperworks of green. These were stout, full-bodied vessels and they were driven hard, out and home across the stormy Atlantic, through every kind of weather that the ocean could throw at a ship. They were fast, and in many cases were said to have been commanded by former privateersmen. In their day, the packets were the one and only means of communication between the United States and Europe, and their masters were exceptional men, to whom were entrusted on voyage after voyage the lives of important persons and the handling of dispatches from government sources, and of mails and specie. They

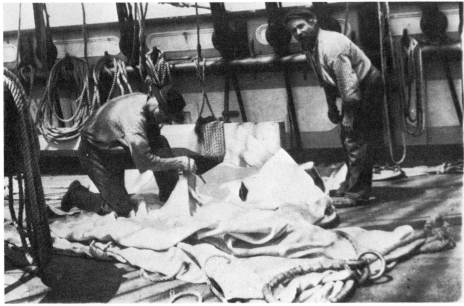

The seafarers who manned the tall ships were as tough as their chosen trade: *above* trying to keep an even keel in a storm; *below* mending sails on the deck of the *Loch Tay*.

Opposite The nineteenth-century clippers were notable for their beauty, grace and speed.

The ladies and gentlemen who were the passengers aboard the tall ships expected to be treated courteously by the master.

had to be thorough seamen, conscientious, men of robust health who could withstand perhaps many days on deck at a stretch as they fought their small commands through storm and cold, ice and snow and fog. They needed exceptional characters and personalities too, these first commanders of the North Atlantic passenger trade: there were rumbustious crews to be controlled with an iron hand, men who very largely were out of British and Continental gaols, while at the other end of the scale were the ladies and gentlemen of the passenger list, who had to be courteously treated with such graces and social airs as could be mustered by a hard-driving ship's master even when cold and soaked to the skin and weary enough to fall asleep where he stood.

The packets carried plenty of sail, and the racing was taken seriously, although in fact fourteen knots was about the maximum they ever achieved as an average speed, and to keep this up involved plenty of 'belaying-pin soup' and 'handspike hash' dished up by the hard-case mates whose job it was to drive the crew. There is ground for saying that these early packet ships produced the first Blue Riband race: in 1837 the Black Ball Line's *Columbus* of 597 tons, under Captain de Peyster, took on the *Sheridan* of the Dramatic Line, Captain Russell in command, on her maiden voyage. The wager was for $10,000 on the run from New York to Liverpool. Both ships sailed together from New York on 2 August, *Columbus* reaching Liverpool Bay in sixteen days and *Sheridan* taking two days longer. This was the first recorded North Atlantic race.

Design

Although the early Baltimore clippers owed their origins to the demands of the War of Independence and the need for small, fast ships to outsail British warships, speed was not, in the early part of the nineteenth century, the first consideration when building a ship. Life itself was easier and slower and altogether more leisurely, and, as ever, the sea tended to follow the fashions and requirements set by the land. The overriding consideration was for cargo-carrying capacity, and it mattered not when the winds might allow that cargo to leave its port and cross the seas – there are instances on record in plenty of great assemblies of ships waiting in river estuaries for the right wind to carry them to sea – and the value of a ship was directly proportional to its possibilities as a cargo-carrier. The fact that England had been largely at war from around the 1760s to 1815 inhibited the improvement of the design of British merchant vessels. This had meant that during those years British ships had been formed into convoys for their protection, and the speed of the convoy was in any case the speed of the slowest ship. It could, no doubt, be truly said that this should have presented a challenge and a spur to the ship designers and builders. Alas, it acted the other way, and seems to have induced a kind of lethargy, almost a case of 'why bother?'; thus the

Americans and the Scandinavian countries gained valuable time over the British, and built ships that had the speed needed for single-ship passages. It was not until peace returned between Britain and France that the desire for fast ships grew, and the British designers began to make up their leeway. Once they did this, the results were excellent, and some very fine ships were produced. Though America had its positive influence on ship design and the advancement towards the clipper, it is possible to exaggerate this; the British designers and builders could hold their own with anybody once they got under way, as it were.

Many factors had their influence upon design, and as the early steamships came along they had their own effect upon later clipper development, with their knifing bows and hollow sections. By the 1850s steam propulsion with its attendant filth and clamour was coming into service, at first by paddle and later by screw, though a full suit of sails was also fitted in such vessels as Brunel's *Great Western*, and the *Great Britain* with her six masts, five of them with fore-and-aft rig and one with square sails, later reduced to three with square rig on all.

In general, even in America, there was opposition to new ideas, largely because the owners, who after all paid the piper in the shape of the designer and builder, were quite often shipmasters themselves, with their own preconceived and very fixed ideas of the shape of a ship. The Californian gold rush in 1849 was a tremendous stimulant to ship design, and vessels in America increased in size to around 1500 tons, with sharp clipper lines and plenty of sail. Everyone was anxious to lay hands on the gold, and anything that floated was wanted to hasten the greedy around the Horn from the east coast – being landsmen, the would-be prospectors were considerably more fearful of the dark interior, with its mountains and deserts, its ferocious Red Indians and its poisonous snakes, than they were of the – to them – as yet unknown Cape Stiff. Meanwhile in Britain clippers were so far rarely built over a mere 500 tons; Britain needed its own stimulus, and when it came with the later discovery of gold in Australia, the British owners and builders, not wishing the good convicts of the Southland to have the wealth all to themselves, pulled their socks up.

The impact of tonnage dues also had an important bearing upon design: design was, and is, always an act of much intricate compromise between economy of running, crewing and handling, of overheads, earning power per voyage, and of the chances for employment to capacity each year. The net result of all this was sometimes to encourage poor design aesthetically, since a fine-lined ship such as a clipper, with thereby less draft and carrying capacity, would necessitate the payment of proportionately much larger sums by way of the various dues – pilotage, berthing, harbourage, lights – than was payable for a wallowing, ungainly bottom that could be stuffed like a sack. Nevertheless, in America the attempts were made, America being the first to become what she

Opposite Terence L. Storey's painting of the Georg Stage; built in 1935 for the 'Georg Stage Memorial Foundation', it is now used as the Danish sail training ship.

The five-masted German square rigger, *Preussen*.

opposite A figurehead was a standard feature of the clippers. The head and left arm of the *Cutty Sark*'s figurehead were lost at sea but this replacement figure was presented by the Canadian Lumberman's Association in 1956.

Photographs taken of the reconstruction of the *Discovery* give us a unique view of the bow and stern timbers between deck.

remained – the land of new ideas and a willingness to experiment and learn.

Sailing ship hulls underwent a quite considerable change over the years, though the alterations in rigging were few, the main standard classifications remaining static at least in basis: the ship rig as already described, the next down the scale being the barque with its three or more masts, (but with no square sail on the mizzen, which was always fore-and-aft rigged) and with a large sail known as the spanker or driver. Brigs had only two masts, never more, never less, and were square-rigged on both, with a gaff-mainsail and a spanker. Combining the advantages of square rig with those of fore-and-aft or schooner rig was the brigantine, having two masts, the fore carrying square rig and the main being

The sleekness of the hull design and the fact that her sails can fill to the wind mark this ship as an example of an extreme clipper.

rigged with fore-and-aft sails; the hermaphrodite brig, again with two masts, was square-rigged as to the foremast while the main carried two square topsails and a spanker. Schooners carried two or more masts with fore-and-aft rig and never any square sail except in the case of a topsail schooner (still seen today, examples being the British Sail Training Association's *Malcolm Miller* and *Sir Winston Churchill*), which in addition to fore-and-aft sails carried square topsails on the foremast, plus gaffsails, the aftermost one of which was extended by a boom.

Virtually all the deep-sea merchant vessels of the nineteenth century were ship-rigged, barque-rigged or schooner-rigged, whether they carried two masts or up to five, as in the case of the German *Preussen*. Their sizes varied very widely indeed, increasing over the years until in 1911 Chantiers de la Gironde produced for Prentoul et Leblond the daddy of them all: the five-masted square-rigged *France II* of 6255 tons and a deadweight capacity of 8000 tons.

In the early days of the clippers there was normally a straight cutwater which raked forward at a fairly sharp angle and terminated in a figurehead set squarely and almost vertically upon it. The stempiece was joined on each side to the hull above the waterline by three or more curving wooden knees known as headrails, and these were strengthened by vertical ties crossing at right angles and floored with curved wooden gratings from whose centre the bowsprit rose. This whole structure was known as the beakhead, and was, as a unit, separate from the hull itself, which was rounded from the beakhead; lower down, near the waterline, the form showed a convex curve. In ships of the latter end of the century the bow had become concave at the waterline, while on deck the lines were almost straight, joining at an acute angle at the stem. The figurehead tended to disappear from the later ships, and the bowsprit to project at a flatter angle. There came some changes, not spectacular ones, to the yards and rigging: the spritsail yard and spritsail topsail vanished; in addition to the bobstays, and extending down from the cap of the bowsprit, a truss for the lower bowsprit stays began to be fitted – the 'dolphin striker' as it was called. In time the bowsprit shrouds became obsolete since the guys that once supported the spritsail yard had been stretched from the hull direct to their supports on the bowsprit proper and the jibboom.

Iron Ships

Vanished also as the years tolled by for sail was the gingerbread work, the splendidly decorated quarter galleries, and the transom. Iron became the builder's medium, and from the end of the 1840s many shipyards were building in both iron and wood. In the first instance wood pure and simple was overtaken by composite-built ships, in which the stem, sternpost, keel and outer planking were built of wood, the frames, beams, floors and keelson of iron. Copper sheathing was fastened to the outer skin to prevent growth of weed and barnacles. The lower masts and topmasts were made of iron, as were the lower yards, while the decks continued to be laid in wood. These ships had great durability; but *Lothair*, 794 tons, built by Walker & Son of London in 1869, was almost the last of them. Iron took over, and in Britain the yards on the Thames, the Mersey, the Tyne and the Clyde were soon hard at work on iron ships, especially on paddlers – in March 1853 thirteen iron sailing ships and only six wooden ones were under construction on the Clyde. Before 1850 most of the iron sailing ships built were schooner-rigged, with some brigs and barques of small tonnage, but from 1852 onwards the trend reversed, with much increased construction of iron full-rigged ships of large sizes and this was to become the established pattern of shipbuilding. From that time on, iron schooners, brigs and brigantines became much less common, with the centre of the shipbuilding business in Britain deserting London for the Mersey – in the Fifties, in fact, London contributed only a single vessel of iron above 900 tons. A wide variety of ships was built in British yards in these middle years, ranging from the fine-lined or extreme clipper *Storm Cloud* to the full-bodied carrier *Aphrodite*. In the Sixties iron became more and more the order of the day and many iron ships were built up to 1500 tons, while in the early Seventies more ships of up to 2000 tons were coming off the ways.

Iron in its turn gave way to steel and indeed from 1858, when the *Ma Roberts*

overleaf The iron shipbuilding works of Mare & Co. at Bow Creek, Blackwall.

(origin of somewhat derogatory name unknown) was built by John Laird for Dr Livingstone, steel got really under way. By 1863 the full-rigged steel ship *Formby* of 1271 tons was built. At this time prices of around £20 per ton were being quoted by the shipbuilders. The launch of the full-rigged ship *Bay of Cadiz* in 1878, by J.G. Thomson of Glasgow, 1700 tons, signalled the final ascendancy of steel. Although the wooden-ship sailors may well have deplored it – and many did – the advent of steel was really an improvement: bigger ships, heavier carriers, much stronger at sea and therefore more preservative of life, they could be as beautiful in their way as the best of the wooden ships.

Before iron and steel replaced the wooden hulls, wood had started to vanish from other parts of the ships: notably the spars and the standing rigging – the shrouds and the stays – and even some of the running rigging. Parts of the sheets where most of the wear came – for instance, at the yardarm sheaves and the quarter blocks – became chain. A lot of the old deck and sail gear disappeared, including the trusses and parrals, and the extended yards meant they could be more closely braced to the wind. It became much easier to stow and reef the upper sails, and the brace-leads were changed, the foreyard and all topmast yards now having their braces led to the ship's sides instead of to stays and shrouds, thus dispensing with many of the leading blocks and reducing the friction always set up when handling sail. This saved both labour and cordage.

Another developing theme was the setting of the foremast farther aft, in the interest of lessening the strain on the hull produced when the bow overhung the trough of a wave: when this happened often, a vessel could eventually become hogged, that is distorted, with her fore part taking a downward bend. When hulls were lengthened it was possible to reposition the foremast, and along with this there came a gradual lessening of the weight of the whole bow section. The shipbuilders Brown and Bell of New York developed a bow shape that was much finer below the waterline. Such was the *Houqua*, built in the early Forties, at which time, so far as the United States were concerned, the building of clippers was reaching its zenith – everyone who had any capital wanted to build, own, sail and race, even a share being better than nothing once the great gold rush had swept America.

In 1845 came *Rainbow*, 750 tons, with its even finer bow, built to John W. Griffiths's specifications by Smith and Dimon of New York. *Rainbow*, with her convex stern and rounded main transom, proved very successful, breaking all records – China and back in seven months under Captain John Land was a splendid example. Griffiths's *Sea Witch* was even faster, and within two to three years a whole fleet of American clippers was taking part in the great China tea trade.

In these mid-century ships a somewhat exaggerated flare of the bows above the water was noted, its purpose being to stop the stem digging itself under a sea and to provide proper buoyancy. The link between this build of bow and the iron windjammers built later in Britain was provided by the *Oriental*, in which the hull was extended to the stem knees, the extended stem being faired into the hull with the result that it cut the water clean and true. Some further raking led to the great clipper ship *Challenge*, built by William Webb in 1851, to which vessel the British very soon replied with *Challenger*. *Challenger* had a very clean bow with all the standing rigging right forward and led through holes in the hull so that all the usual clutter of associated gear had been cut away. Her designer, Donald McKay, had an immense influence on vessels of the mid-nineteenth century. A highly intelligent man, he had been taught his trade by John Griffiths, and in 1826 had come south to New York to join Brown and Bell and Isaac Webb; by 1840 he had progressed to a partnership designing vessels at Newburyport, Massachusetts; and five years later was in Boston working on packets for fast runs, in a city whose merchants tended towards the fuller lines that were a part and parcel of a decent profit-making carrier space. Donald McKay changed the Boston shipbuilding scene very considerably, designing extremely handsome clippers of great length, among them the noted flier *Flying Cloud* of 1851, which held the record of sailing twice from New York to San Francisco around Cape Horn – the notorious east-west passage – each time in 89 days. Of 1783 net register tons *Flying Cloud* was 232 feet long with a beam of 41 feet and a hold depth of 21 feet. McKay built for British owners also: in the 1850s James Baines, the great Liverpool ship owner who ran the Black Ball Line, placed orders for *Lightning*, *Champion of the Seas*, *James Baines* and, a compliment to the builder, *Donald McKay*, each of 2500 tons, for the Australian passenger trade. *Champion of the Seas* made a record run of 465 nautical miles in one day, from noon to noon on 11 to 12 December 1854. McKay was the builder of other noted ships of the day, such as *Empress of the Seas* and *Romance of the Seas*.

Unfortunately the very length alone of some of the American clippers was to contribute in the later years to their eclipse: the growing expense of running such ships was to a great extent due to the fact that it was necessary to build up the keelson inside the ship so as to increase the longitudinal strength, and this very greatly reduced the cargo spaces. The heyday of clipper building in America was in fact short, no more than the fifteen years to 1860, from which time the ships had their rigs much reduced and were built with much more of an eye to their cargo capacity and with less insistence on speed and beauty of line: the beast of profit was taking over fast. In both the United States and Britain, though often the spars were reduced in size to keep down costs, mainly crew costs, the vessels themselves grew bigger and bigger until the tonnage average was well over the 1000 mark, while the *Sovereign of the Seas* at 2421 tons – she was dismasted off the Horn on her maiden voyage – and Donald McKay's *Great Republic* at no less than 4357 tons, were giants of their day.

The latter, built in 1853 as the then biggest sailing ship in the world – her main truck was 228 feet above the deck – and the only clipper to have four masts in place of the usual three, was in fact less successful than McKay's earlier work, though he himself regarded her as his masterpiece; but her launch from the Boston yard, on 4 October 1853, was a nine days' wonder. No less than sixty thousand good citizens came to watch and wish the *Great Republic* godspeed, the day being declared a public holiday. Longfellow wrote a poem in honour of the occasion. Splendid indeed she was, with her great golden eagle proudly decorating her stem, a fifteen-horsepower steam engine to work her winches, and crewed by a magnificent one hundred seamen and thirty boys. Destined for the Australian run, she made her first short trip to New York under the command of her builder's brother, Captain Lauchlan McKay, but in New York she attracted sparks from the premises of the Novelty Baking Company, and, sadly, was burned to the water's edge. She spent a year undergoing repairs, but was diverted from the Australian run to the Crimea, where the British were at war with Russia, to act as a troopship. Later she was to act as such again in the American Civil War.

The United States produced some first-class schooner-rigged vessels over the years. These craft, of three, four, five and six masts, and one of seven, the *Thomas W. Lawson* built as late as 1902, handled quite differently from square rig, and the square-rig seamen were never happy aboard the schooners, with their massive swinging booms sweeping across the deck to maim and kill and cast overboard into raging seas. Most of the work was done from the deck, with the assistance of steam winches, and steam from the donkey boiler was mostly available at sea except at such times as bad weather put out the fires, or fires were drawn by order of the master as a safety precaution in heavy seas. Steam winches were used to hoist sail and to work the lifts and downhauls of the staysails, to clew up gaff-topsails and to furl the large gaffsails. Lines running vertically from the lifts and known as 'Lazy Jacks' served this purpose, and there was little necessity for men to go aloft. The longest wooden vessel ever built was the six-masted schooner *Wyoming*, constructed at Bath, Maine, for owners in New York. She had a length of 330 feet, thus beating McKay's *Great Republic* by some six feet.

It is worth noting here that the average speed of the clippers was probably around fourteen to fifteen knots, though much higher speeds have been noted: *Lightning* had made nineteen knots, *James Baines* twenty-one; while *Cutty Sark*, built for speed on the China tea run, clocked up a maximum of 17.5 knots. *Cutty Sark*, built on the Clyde in 1869, 212 feet long and with a beam of 36 feet, was driven

This photograph of the American schooner-rigged *Wyoming* was taken on 29 February 1924 as she sailed down Chesapeake Bay; she was lost at sea a few days later.

through wind and weather by a plain sail area of 32,000 square feet, and although not exceptionally fast was a classic among the great sailing ships of all time. Incidentally, if all her rope was laid end to end, it would have covered more than ten miles.

Although in the closing years of the century, as sail itself began to approach its close, the seas were dominated by increasing numbers of steamers, they were also sailed by the great grain carriers of the Australian trade, and the wool ships, and the vessels running nitrates from Chilean ports. The grain ships, steel-built, ships and barques of 2000 tons in many cases, were unwieldy and slow, the windjammers that had literally to be 'jammed' into the wind and needed a skill and sailing technique different from the skills required to handle the clippers. Such were the four-masted barques *Sutherlandshire* of Glasgow's Shire Lines, and *Loudoun Hill* of the J.R. Dickson Line, also of Glasgow; and the *Lancing*, built in 1865 as a mail steamer, which actually made the very unusual, though not unique, conversion to sail in 1888.

The Builders

The men who built the great ships of the nineteenth century have an immortal niche in maritime history. Donald McKay, already referred to, was perhaps the best known of them all, but there were many others who had a profound influence upon ship design and construction. William H. Webb of New York was considered in the Fifties to be America's foremost shipbuilder, and in addition to the great *Challenge* was responsible for the extreme clipper *Flying Dutchman*, and the packets *America* and *Australia* for the Black Star Line. In 1853 he built the *Young America* at a cost of $140,000, a ship of a very racy build, and exceptionally strong. She had three decks, and her poop, 42 feet in length, contained very well fitted-out passenger accommodation. In December 1868 *Young America* under Captain Cummings, carrying a tricky cargo of railway iron, was taken aback by a pampero, a cold wind that storms down into the South Atlantic from the Andes mountains, and was thrown on to her beam ends. The axes had just been ordered to the weather lanyards when the mizzen topmast went, taking the main topgallant and fore royal masts with it. Although Monte Video was handy by, Captain Cummings decided not to accept the long delay for repairs but to carry on around Cape Horn, even though the ship was making water. After some desperately hard work in atrocious weather, with the pampero tearing at the ship, the pumps going continuously, and his crew at times on the verge of mutiny, Cummings had the mizzen jury-rigged; with the main topgallant mast fidded, he brought his ship round the pitch of the Horn in easier weather to make San Francisco and a very well-deserved hero's welcome almost two months later.

The *Lancing*, a steamer which was later converted to sail.

Another noted shipbuilder was Stephen Smith. Born in Connecticut, he joined with John Dimon to found the firm of Smith and Dimon. He built the packet ships *Roscoe* and *Independence*, and some of the North River steamboats. Jacob A. Westervelt, born in New Jersey in 1800, was himself the son of a shipbuilder. He went to sea before the mast, and when he came ashore served an apprenticeship with Christian Bergh, becoming a partner and retiring as early as 1837; but after a tour of Europe he was back in harness and built more ships at Williamsburg.

One of the best known of the naval architects in terms of clipper design was John Rennie, a Scotsman. Rennie built the schooner *Florence* at Aberdeen in 1831, but moved to Canada towards the end of the Thirties, establishing a shipyard at Bathurst, New Brunswick; here he designed the barques *Beraza* and *Raphael*, both of them very fast sailers, built to his specifications by Joseph Cunard of Miramichi for London owners. Returning to Britain in the late Forties, Rennie settled in Liverpool and joined forces with John Johnson to found the firm of Rennie, Johnson and Company, shipbuilders, at Brunswick Dock. The firm went bankrupt in 1855 after building some fine ships, including the wooden ship *Margaret Deane*, the barque *Sappho*, and the frigate *Earl of Eglinton*, a 1270-ton vessel built of oak and teak. In that final year before bankruptcy Rennie completed two steamers and four sailers. *Fiery Cross*, a wooden clipper of 788 tons and a future record breaker, was under construction when the firm went out of business. During the Sixties Rennie produced the tea clippers *Black Prince* and *Norman Court*, also the auxiliary steamer *Sea King*, later to find fame as the Confederate cruiser *Shenandoah* in the American Civil War.

The firm of Robert Steele of Greenock was one of the 'greats' of the day. Their first clipper was the *Kate Carnie*, though William Steele, the firm's designer, had had a good deal of experience of fast ships and yachts before this. By the Sixties Robert Steele's grandsons were noted for their fine, fast clippers built for the China trade, and indeed they were the builders of the famous clipper ship *Taeping* which raced *Ariel* neck-and-neck for home from the China seas in 1866.

Accommodation

The sailing qualities of the vessels these builders produced was well matched by the elegance of the accommodation, at least so far as the officers were concerned. Throughout the whole of the nineteenth century and later, there was a vast difference between the fo'c'sle hands and the afterguard; the former, lying in their tiered bunks in the gloomy darkness of their leaky, smelly cavern mostly (in the older vessels) right forward in the eyes of the ship, no doubt looked enviously upon the more spacious life of the master and mates, at any rate in the later ships. In the big steel-built windjammers the officers' quarters were given the best of the joiner's and the cabinet-maker's skill; there was polished teak panelling in the saloon and cabins, beautifully made doors and skylights, glass racks and decanter holders to grace the great table at meals and hold water and wine steady against the heave of restless seas. The British and American ships went in for much decoration, restrained and tasteful and never flamboyant, and the saloons were comfortable places with their stoves, even fireplaces in some ships, revolving chairs, well-upholstered sofas, and the rich panelling. Spirit lamps hung from the deckheads, not smoking thanks to the constant proper attention of the lamp-trimmer, but swaying endlessly to the roll of the ship. The decks were carpeted, and as like as not there would be small children playing, their mother, the captain's wife, perhaps sewing away on the sofa; for often the captains would take their wives and young families to sea with them and the scene in the saloon could be a very domestic one. Frequently in the case of those captains who owned their ships, the ship was home and in effect they were sea gypsies in a sea caravan.

The cabins and saloon lay beneath the poop, right aft, where the master was handy for the wheel and the officer of the watch when wanted in an emergency. Forward of the poop would be the petty officers' deckhouse, often with the standard compass on its roof since, in the iron and steel vessels, this was found to be the best position to maintain equilibrium against the ship's inbuilt magnetic attraction, known as deviation. Access could be made from the deck or from the

The saloon of the passenger sailing ship *Harbinger*, built in 1876; the black mass in the centre is the mizzen.

fore-and-aft, or flying, bridges which ran above the deck from poop to fo'c'sle. Next, between the fore and main masts would be the main deckhouse, where the galley and boilerhouse would be situated; also the donkey engine and, in ships not berthing the hands under the fo'c'sle-head, the crew's accommodation. The galley was a narrow compartment wedged between the bunkhouse and the boiler, a narrow passage into which all too often the sea would rush and thunder, dousing fire and food and cook. The latter had perhaps the most unenviable job aboard the ship: it was second nature for all hands to complain about the efforts of the cook, customarily known as Slushy. In all truth, his available ingredients were few and repetitious: ship's biscuit treated in a variety of ways, salt pork from casks usually with enormous worms crawling through, and few vegetables to be seen after the first couple of days out from port. A little freshness would be provided by chickens and eggs from the hencoop, and often there would be cows and pigs undergoing the torture of roaring seas and wind until their time for slaughter came.

In the crew's sleeping quarters, lots were drawn for the best bunks: upper, lower, near the stove, away from the door that admitted the great long rollers, or Cape Horn greybeards, inside berth or out. Beneath the bottom layer of bunks were stowed the sea chests, lashed to ringbolts in the deck to prevent them taking charge in a seaway. In these chests lay each man's home, his very life. He had nothing else aboard the ship to call his own, and often enough the sea chest was an anchorage for a seasick, homesick youth upon the traumatic experience of his first voyage: inside the lid there would probably be photographs of home and mother, and these were kinder, happier things to look upon than the first mate. There is a yarn, a true one, about the first mate of a windjammer, an Iredale and Porter ship out of Liverpool for Australia, running down the Irish Sea for the Fastnet, with a first-voyage apprentice bringing his stomach up in the scuppers. Up comes the mate, bearing in his hand a chunk of salt pork attached to a piece of string; the apprentice is hauled to his feet by the scruff of his neck, his mouth forced open, the salt pork thrust in and down by the tobacco-stained and tarry finger of the mate. Once down, the pork is withdrawn again upon its string. 'Now', says the mate, 'you'll be so god-damn sick you'll never be sick again hereafter.'

Across the living quarters would be strung the clotheslines upon which the crew would hope to dry out sea-soaked gear, though in fact this was seldom possible in bad weather; water always got into the deckhouse, admitted either as men came in and out through the door, or forced in by wind and waves that shattered doors on occasions like matchwood; the least that could be expected, maybe for days on end, was a constant surge back and forth of scummy water across the deck.

Deck Gear

Aft of the main deckhouse in the big steel ships there would probably be a distillation unit to provide water for the boiler and for drinking; the men sailing in such well-fitted ships were lucky. In earlier vessels the water came aboard in barricoes, or breakers, and was guarded like Fort Knox, and whenever there was rain the spare canvas would be rigged on deck to catch what might, on a long voyage, prove to be a life-saving last drop. In any event, the water from the barricoes was best taken in strong Scotch whisky, if there was any, as the run progressed.

Going forward along the waist, the windlass gear for working the anchors would be found just aft of the break of the fo'c'sle, with the anchors themselves well lashed down on the fo'c'sle itself whilst at sea. Small sheers on deck were used to swing out the anchors to the catheads before letting go upon arrival in an anchorage. Under the fo'c'sle itself were the store-rooms, smelly and ill-lit compartments containing paint, lamp material, petrol, deck gear of pulleys, blocks and tackles, rope, canvas, wash-deck equipment such as swabs and scrubbers, and an assortment of tow bungs, rags, oil, grease and carpenter's tools. A part of the space in the fore part of the ship was usually allotted to the eatable livestock, which, in addition to the cows and pigs aforementioned, might well include a sheep or two for the saloon. On deck most vessels carried four boats, tarpaulin-covered against the seas and held griped-in to davits; on the starboard side would be a fifth boat in cradles, ready to slip at a moment's notice in an emergency such as 'man overboard'; on the port side there would be a whaler, also for use as a lifeboat when required.

Spaced along the upper deck were the cargo hatches, with their heavy covers of reinforced hardwood planks, well chocked in and secured with three separate layers of tarpaulin held down with ropes and more chocks, to withstand the pounding weight of heavy seas. Below the hatches lay the reason for the ship's presence upon the sea, her cargo, to be held inviolate against nature and disaster, against the fire that could come from a self-combustible cargo such as wool, or a cargo that could swell when it met water, such as rice, which on more than one occasion in the long story of the sea swelled and in its irresistible pressures split the sides of holds like paper and sank the ship in minutes.

3

Farewell to England

LOWER masts and bowsprit of iron, lad, lower yards steel. Topmasts, t'gallantmasts and tops'l yards are good Vancouver pine and all other spars pitch pine. We've no donkey boiler and all the work's done by hand. Bracing the yards isn't funny, with the decks awash up to a man's shoulder.'

In such terms might any first-voyage apprentice be addressed, probably with less politeness and a good deal more pungency, when taken on his first gawping tour of his strange and frightening new world of wood, canvas, rope and hard-living men. To the first voyager, the cobweb of ropes was a nightmare: some three hundred different ones – sheets, brails, halliards, downhauls, braces for the various sails – each with its own name and special function, and woe betide the hand that pulled the wrong one. Inside two to three months, the young apprentice would be expected to go unerringly for the right and proper one in darkness with a full gale blowing the sea into fury along the deck.

The introductory tour of familiarization with what at times would be hell on earth would usually take place after the youth had been shown his quarters in the deckhouse, where, with perhaps half-a-dozen other apprentices of varying seniority, he would be berthed little better than the hands before the mast. The apprentices would share one half of the deckhouse, the other half being occupied by the petty officers – bosun, sailmaker, carpenter, cook. The first voyager's mentor would more than likely be the senior apprentice, a demigod nearly out of his time and about to sit his Board of Trade examination for second mate; the bosun would be too busy, the second mate likewise, the first mate rather too distant, and the master unapproachable other than by fools who might rush in begging for their heads to be bitten off. The days of the great sailing ships were not democratic ones, and men who had earned their positions by years of breakingly hard work and sweat and danger knew their own value and importance in the social scale – and were accorded it unstintingly.

It took much time to rise to command. Youths wishing to take the examinations for their professional certificates of competency in British ships – once standards of seagoing qualifications had been laid down by the Mercantile Marine Act of 1850 – had to undergo four years' sea time aboard a 'deepwater' vessel, a vessel going foreign outside home trade limits. And four years' sea time meant what it said: time in port, time between ships, was deducted. After those four years the apprentice could sit for second mate; after another two, for mate; and after another year, for his certificate of competency as master – after which it would probably be many more years before the newly-qualified master mariner was actually appointed to his first command. Small wonder that when he was he walked like God, small wonder that he was an autocrat who demanded, and always got, instant obedience. His word was absolute law, and he ruled the lives and destinies of his crew in every detail of their existence, representing as he did

opposite This apparent maze of ropes is actually the tidy, orderly rigging of a tall ship.

Won at a cost of many hard years at sea, the highly prized certificate of competency as master.

a combination of squire, policeman, doctor, judge and jury, physical saviour in times of danger, paymaster, all-provider and even marriage guidance counsellor.

The masters who took the square-riggers to sea were a breed all on their own, with no single shore-side counterpart below the monarch, men who were able to take total responsibility for lives and a valuable ship and cargo and to drive that responsibility hard through the world's heaving oceans, through storm and frustrating calm, through blinding blizzards and the heat of tropic suns, the icy cold of the Southern Ocean and the sticky heat of the Bay of Bengal or the West African coast. And they possessed in most cases the characteristics and eccentricities to go with such autocracy: there is a story of one master sailing regularly in Iredale and Porter's ships from the Mersey to South American ports and Australia whose practice it was to buy a brand-new tall hat on each arrival home in Liverpool, and then, the night before moving out again for sea on his next voyage, to cast the hat ceremoniously into the Mersey, signifying that dressing-up was finished until his ship next came home.

The Owners
Liverpool was a sailor's town if ever there was one, being to the British Merchant Service what the dockyard towns of Portsmouth, Devonport and Chatham were

to the Navy. Contemporary accounts speak eloquently of the seafaring character of the city washed by the Mersey, of its public houses and brothels, its roistering sailors from every port and ocean in the world getting rid of hard-earned cash on wine, women and song. As a sailor's town, Liverpool was also a shipowner's town. Tall and imposing buildings proclaimed on their well-polished brass plates names that were respected the world over: Brocklebank, Bibby, Lamport, Holt, Castle Line, Cunard. John Bibby had started in business by running a small fleet of packet ships between Parkgate and Dublin before establishing his service to Alexandria and later across the North Atlantic. William Lamport and George Holt founded their firm in 1845. Charles MacIver started a connection with the Mediterranean out of Liverpool in 1851 with one ship; his trading with this vessel was so successful that Samuel Cunard and George Burns joined him, and thus was created the Cunard service to the Levant.

Cunard, an American of German descent, was born in Halifax, Nova Scotia, of a Quaker family, and proved to be a young man of determination and great energy, inclined to impetuosity, and often of a demanding manner. He left employment in Halifax dockyard in order to help found the family firm of Abraham Cunard and Sons, with interests in the timber export trade, but price-cutting in a keen business left the firm defeated and Samuel developed along his own paths, landing a mail contract for his sailing ships from Halifax to Bermuda. He became interested in the British end of the shipping business when, whilst visiting England, the British East India Company gave him their agency for

Queen's Dock, Liverpool, in the nineteenth century.

Halifax. Unfortunately for the sailing ships, however, Samuel Cunard was attracted towards the new era of steam rather than to sail.

Later, Lamport and Holt were to set up their connection with the River Plate in South America. Trade grew by leaps and bounds, going in many directions and vastly increasing the significance of the port of Liverpool. After the repeal of the Corn Laws by Sir Robert Peel in 1846, Russia was developed as a source of grain supply, while during the cotton famine in the Sixties an active trade grew in cotton from Egypt, imported through Alexandria. In 1845 Wilson and Pilkington started as shipbrokers; their first White Star ship sailed four years later. In 1864 Robert Alexander, together with Liston, Young and Company of London, started a sailing ship service to India and Australia, going into steam in 1871 and creating the Sun Steam Ship Company, which later became the Hall Line. Donald, later Sir Donald, Currie, a Greenock Scot educated in Belfast, founded in 1862 the Castle Line to Calcutta, later being drawn into the South African trade and becoming part of Union Castle. Currie had been interested in shipping from boyhood, and from 1844 to 1862 was employed by Cunard, starting right at the bottom and becoming head of Cunard's cargo department before being sent to open up branches in France to initiate trade between that country and America.

A number of American companies used Liverpool as a turn-round port. There was a regular transatlantic service maintained from 1816 by the American Black Ball Line, which ran two ships of 500 tons twice a month – on the 1st and 16th – from Liverpool; and it was in fact American initiative that helped Liverpool to break down the Bristol and London monopoly as terminal ports for the North Atlantic passenger traffic. The Black Ball sailing packets made the Liverpool to New York run in forty days, and New York to Liverpool in twenty-three. An exceptional run was made by the *Canada*, which on one occasion took only 15 days 18 hours on the New York to Liverpool run. The passage was greatly speeded up as time went on, and for many years the American packets dominated the emigrant trade, each of their ships carrying between 500 and 700 passengers, those travelling in the steerage paying from £3 to £5 and each passenger buying his own food and cooking it himself. (The American Black Ball Line is not, of course, to be confused with the Black Ball Line to Australia founded by James Baines, the Liverpool man born behind his mother's cake shop in Upper Duke Street, who rose to control no less than eighty-six ships, employing 300 officers and 3000 seamen, before he was bankrupted by steam and died in a common lodging house.)

The London and Newfoundland-based firm of C.T. Bowring owes its origins to the American sailing ships: Benjamin Bowring, its founder, had opened a British branch in Liverpool in 1830. Enoch Train's White Diamond Line traded between Liverpool and Boston, starting its sailings in 1839 and later becoming a British company with Liverpool as its headquarters. Another American who made

Liverpool his base was William Brown, the founder of Brown, Shipley and
Company. The firm fell on bad times as a result of the war of 1812 between the
United States and Britain, but after the ending of the Napoleonic Wars did so well
that Brown stayed on in Liverpool to make his fortune. This he did so effectively
that not only was he knighted by the British monarch but also became a colonel
in a British regiment, the Liverpool Volunteers.

Across the Atlantic between the East and Hudson Rivers were the great
indigenous shipowners of New York. In the early days of the century, Quakers
were prominent in the business of running ships: an instance was Isaac Wright, a
merchant of Long Island and an importer of textiles from Britain. Isaac brought
in his son William as a partner, along with Francis Thompson, another Quaker
who had come to New York for the purpose of marketing woollen goods made
by his father and brother in Yorkshire, England. By 1816 they had been joined by

Masts dominated the skyline of New
York's North River in the 1870s.

yet another Quaker, Jeremiah Thompson, the nephew of Francis. Jeremiah, who
was a notable importer of woollen goods, also exported raw cotton from the
southern states to Liverpool. Making up the number of the partnership to five
was Benjamin Marshall, another Yorkshireman, engaged in the import of cotton
manufactures from Lancashire and, again, the export of raw cotton. The
partnership started with one ship, the *Pacific*, of 384 tons, which traded regularly
between New York and Liverpool, but soon came the addition of *Amity*, *Courier*
and *James Monroe* and the establishment of a full transatlantic service.

It is of interest to note that when, as in the case of the Quaker partnership,
several individuals jointly owned a ship or ships, one of them usually acted as
ship's husband, a post to some extent comparable with that of Marine
Superintendent of the Line today. The duties of ship's husband involved the
appointment and instructions of masters, making decisions in regard to repairs,
handling the custom house requirements for entering and clearing ships, finding
and contracting cargoes and the ordering of the vessel's seagoing career. In such
ways did the old-time owners take an active, personal part in the running of their
businesses: remoteness on the part of the Board was virtually unknown, and it is
probably true to state that it was the personal touch that inspired the great
traditions of loyalty and service to be found, almost to a man, among the masters
and mates and petty officers of the great sailing ships, a tradition of service that,
spreading out from South Street – which was the base of the principal shipowners
and site of the offices of the most noteworthy foreign packets – put New York
firmly on the map of world shipping. South Street was well placed: running
along the East River, the owners' and agents' windows looked straight onto the
East River piers and their clustered forests of masts and spars, bowsprits and
jibbooms, all of them close and instant reminders of distant seas and foreign lands
and of the seaborne trade that linked those lands and oceans to the port of New
York.

By the middle of the nineteenth century, New York was second only to
London in its volume of shipping, though in fact Liverpool had a larger volume
of commerce to its credit; and by 1850 the tonnage handled in and out of New
York was greater than the combined tonnage handled in Boston, Baltimore, New
Orleans and Philadelphia. Trade had been on the increase since the turn of the
century. Following the successes of the Quaker partnership, in 1821 Thomas Cope
of Philadelphia started his line of packets to Liverpool with the ships *Lancaster* of 290
tons and *Tuscarora* of 379 tons. These were followed by larger vessels, some of them
the fastest and smartest in the North Atlantic trade. Also in 1821 the Red Star Line
was established to run from New York to Liverpool, with the *Panther*, *Meteor*,
Hercules, and the second *Manhattan*. Shortly after this came the Swallow Tail Line
founded by Grinnell, Minturn and Company, who later established their London

Line. A good year for shipping was 1821: two cousins, John and Charles Griswold, made a significant contribution to the port of New York with their Black X packets to London. In 1831 the New Orleans Line began sailing its packets *Nashville*, *Huntsville*, *Creole* and *Natchez* out of New York, these vessels being the first poop-decked packets. In 1836 came the Dramatic Line, sailing the ships *Siddons*, *Shakespeare*, *Garrick* and *Roscius* on the Liverpool run. All these Dramatic liners were of around 700 tons, which at that time was considered fully large enough for the Atlantic trade. New York was coming up fast: in 1825 the Erie Canal had been opened, and as a result pushed New York towards its great position in the world of shipping. With the enormous boost given to commerce by the canal, New York became the great entry port of the United States' eastern seaboard.

Emigration
For much of the nineteenth century the North Atlantic trade was concerned with the great tide of emigrants that flowed out of Britain and the Continental countries of Europe and even of Asia. Many of those emigrants came from Ireland, many from Scotland, and by far the larger part of the British emigration was channelled through the port of Liverpool. Much business came to the shipping companies whose house flags adorned Water Street and other famous thoroughfares, flags that drooped limply under the grey Mersey drizzle that so often dampened the pavements and sent shipping clerks and messengers scurrying for the dry security of their chest-high desks, a suitable welcome for the depressed men and women from the wreathing mists and rain of Killarney and Galway, Mayo and Cork. Over all would be the distinctive smell of old Liverpool: the smell that met the Irish packets from Dublin's North Wall as they brought their human cargoes in past the great warehouses – a magic mixture of mist and soot and tar laced like the Thames with the fragrance of spices from the East, and with the funnel-smoke of steamers, dirty monsters that were beginning to fill the skies with their fumes.

With its eventual 1614 acres of docks and 36 miles of quays, Liverpool was, after London, the chief seaport of Britain, and by the end of the century the tonnage owned in the port exceeded the tonnage of all the German empire and was three times the overseas tonnage owned by the United States. The great Liverpool landing stage was built in 1847, and enlarged in 1874 and again in 1897 in order to cope with the enormous passenger traffic from the Mersey ferries, the coastal shipping and the ever-larger ocean liners. It was all a far cry from a Scottish clachan by a quiet lochside, far from the peaceful if blighted green fields and purple-brown turf bogs of Ireland – but the impact of the great commercial city must have been less of a shock than the embarkation aboard the emigrant ships for North America.

Opposite A detail of Brooking's *An Indiaman in A Fresh Breeze*; before the heyday of the clippers, East Indiamen were the preferred merchant vessel.

The *Shakespeare* at Cape Town.

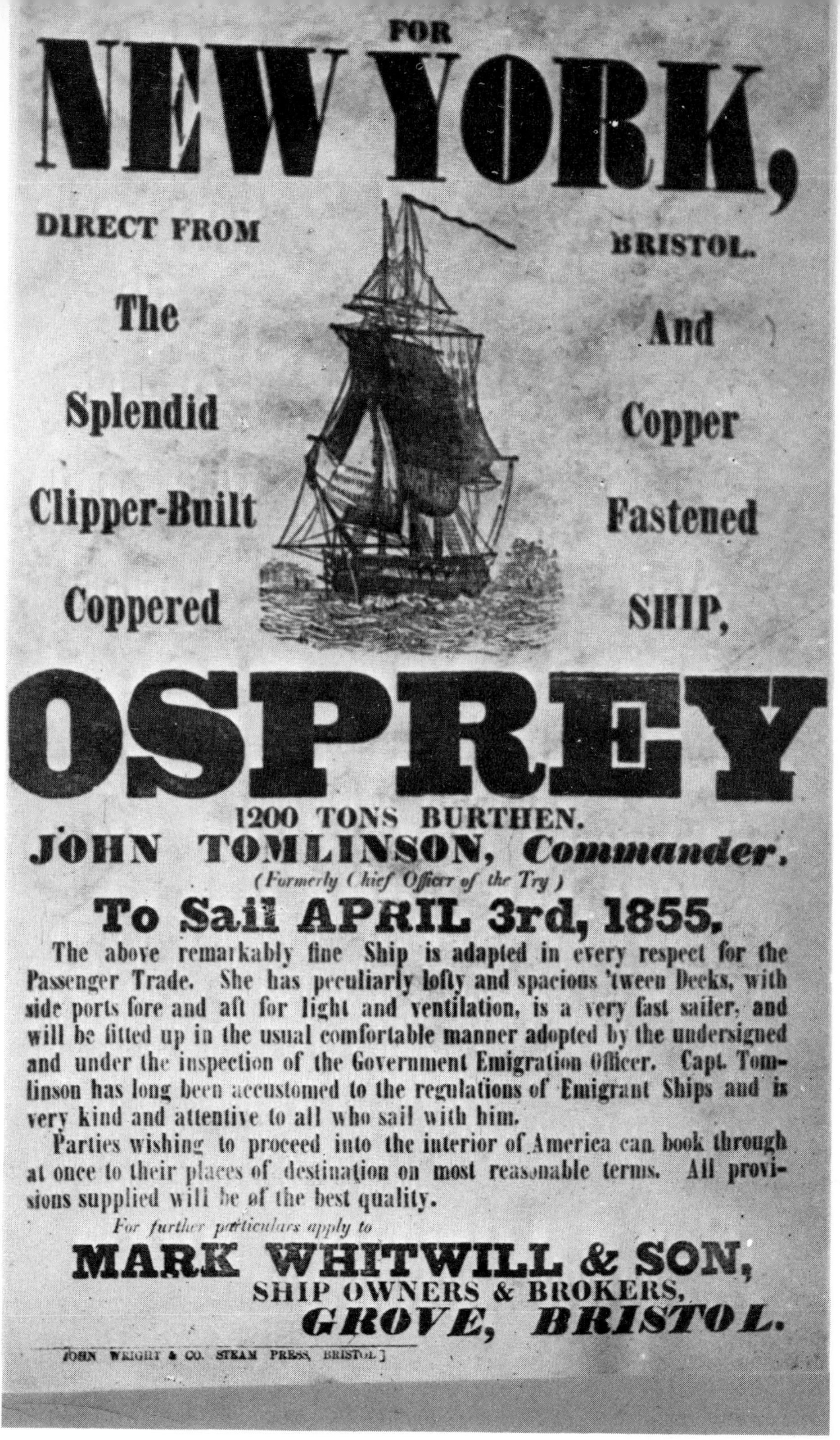

Assurances to potential passengers of
the *Osprey*.

FOR NEW YORK,

DIRECT FROM   BRISTOL.

The   And

Splendid   Copper

Clipper-Built   Fastened

Coppered   SHIP,

OSPREY

1200 TONS BURTHEN.
JOHN TOMLINSON, Commander,
(Formerly Chief Officer of the Try)

To Sail APRIL 3rd, 1855,

The above remarkably fine Ship is adapted in every respect for the
Passenger Trade. She has peculiarly lofty and spacious 'tween Decks, with
side ports fore and aft for light and ventilation, is a very fast sailer, and
will be fitted up in the usual comfortable manner adopted by the undersigned
and under the inspection of the Government Emigration Officer. Capt. Tomlinson has long been accustomed to the regulations of Emigrant Ships and is
very kind and attentive to all who sail with him.

Parties wishing to proceed into the interior of America can book through
at once to their places of destination on most reasonable terms. All provi-
sions supplied will be of the best quality.

For further particulars apply to

MARK WHITWILL & SON,
SHIP OWNERS & BROKERS,
GROVE, BRISTOL.

JOHN WRIGHT & CO. STEAM PRESS, BRISTOL.

Between 1819 and 1859 no less than five million persons had gone to the United
States alone from Europe; between 1846 and 1860 half a million went to Canada
from Britain, and mostly they travelled in extreme discomfort and deprivation. It
was the establishment by the Black Ball Line of sailing packets of the first regular
Liverpool–New York service that made Liverpool, over the next few years, the
main port of departure for Irish, Scottish and English emigrants, as well as of
considerable numbers of Germans and Norwegians using Britain as a stepping
stone on their journey from their own lands. So far as Britain was concerned, the

emigrant trade really took off when in 1825 the anti-emigration laws were repealed, and as a result official recognition was at last given to what everyone had known already – that the country was greatly overpopulated in relation to the work available. In 1830 the revolt in Poland led to very heavy emigration from that country, and in America Congress allotted parcels of public land for Polish settlement. Then in 1840 Samuel Cunard founded his famous steamship line, consisting of four ships which were to constitute the first serious threat to sail and also to the *Great Western* which used both sail and steam. Cunard's ss *Britannia* left Liverpool on 4 July 1840 and obtained the highly-prized mail contract, which was worth £60,000, a great deal of money in those days, in return for guaranteeing thirty Atlantic crossings per year.

In 1846 there were disastrous crop failures in Germany and Holland, and the subsequent mortgage foreclosures and forced sales sent tens of thousands of emigrants to the United States. This was followed in 1846–7 by the Irish potato famine, when thousands died of starvation and a huge proportion of those left alive decided to emigrate. Even substantial farmers gave up the Irish ghost, and along with their cottagers and labourers joined the human tide flowing across the Atlantic. In the first part of the nineteenth century the emigration to America was mostly of Irish and Germans; in the second part Italians and East Europeans; between 1845 and 1860 a million Germans reached America, including many students and intellectuals. There were also many political refugees from other countries: Bohemians, Poles, Hungarians who had been defeated in their struggle for freedom in 1848. From 1870 to the end of the century another eleven million persons went to America, including even Chinese, who were not very popular except as cooks in the lumber camps, where a great many Scandinavians had gone to live and work, felling timber in the great north-west. By the end of the century North America had absorbed and was still absorbing huge armies of Italians, Russians, Poles, Czechs, Hungarians, Rumanians, Bulgarians, Austrians and Greeks.

Masters and Mates

On the voyage across, the early settlers at least had known the rigours and horrors of an unaccustomed sea life. Discipline at sea was of necessity iron-hard and rigid. Any first mate who aspired to the grandeur and dignity of the tall hat and the masters' room in the owners' offices had to run smart, fast and efficient ships. One owner of those days, chairman of a family line, son of the last chairman, father and grandfather of the next two in succession, had dreamed up a word for throwing at youths who wished for the honour of an apprenticeship in his line. The word was 'Jodurecom', and it signified that a job meant Duty, Responsibility, fitness to Command. That owner used to elaborate: the emphasis

overleaf The *Great Western* leaving Kingroad on her maiden voyage in 1837.

was on duty throughout; the young aspirant must be attentive and obedient to every order of the master. The master's whim was his command. Aboard any vessel at sea, from the smallest fishing smack to the enormous coal-burning steamships of Samuel Cunard, the master – whose official status under British Board of Trade terminology was in fact Master Under God – was the supreme authority, overriding the Line itself, the Board and even the Chairman. For the duration of Articles, which was to say for the duration of the voyage, the vessel was legally and in all respects delivered into the hands of its master and ceased to be the property of the Line – though woe betide any master who took this legal provision too literally and failed to hand it back!

The Articles of Agreement themselves formed a contract on duties and wages made between the master and his crew, not between the Board and the crew. The master was legally liable for all disbursements and expenses, including payment to the crew – though, again, any shipping company that defaulted when presented with the master's reckoning would soon find no officers to sail its ships. It was a matter of mutual trust and respect; the master was there not only to sail and command his ship but also to represent the commercial interests of the owners. He took administrative as well as executive charge of the voyage, having often, in ports where the owners did not maintain an agency, to negotiate for homeward freight; it was often entirely up to the master as to whether or not the homeward run would pay, and it was his responsibility to argue the terms of the contract, as it was to make the purchases of food for the crew and equipment for the ship on the best terms available to him. Immediate decisions were the master's lot: at sea to save life, ashore to save cost – whether or not to enter a port for repairs to damage sustained, a balance to be struck between delays incurred thereby and the possible risk to men, ship and cargo by keeping to the seas and making good with the ship's resources. Always decisions, and always on duty until the Articles expired. There was a story of the master of the ship *Maria Rickmers*, whose ship took eighty-two days on passage from Barry Roads in South Wales to Singapore. It had been a terrible voyage of filthy weather and hardship and when, on bringing his ship safely to port, the exhausted master was handed a cable from his owners expressing not their gratitude for a safe arrival but their disappointment in his long run, shock and indignation caused him to fall dead upon his own deck.

Masters in sail carried an immense responsibility across the seas, and the Line expected them to live up to very high standards of efficiency and personal behaviour. Drink, though taken, and often copiously, ashore, was usually carefully controlled at sea: a reference to sobriety or otherwise was customarily to be found in every master's report on his officers. The profession of the sea was exacting and rough, and it was not only the crew that had to be attentive to the

The *Maria Rickmers* – a ship which survived the perils of the sea but whose delayed run indirectly resulted in her master's death.

wishes and demands of the master. 'Under God' was a somewhat all-embracing term, and it included the passengers, a category of which the steerage-class emigrants formed, like midshipmen of the Royal Navy, the lowest form of animal life to be found at sea.

Passengers

In the stirring years of empire-building and of great endeavour, passengers were not as passengers became in the heyday of Cunard-White Star between the two world wars. No discreet steward pandered deferentially to their every whim – whims were the sole prerogative of the master; no gold-encrusted figure, majestic in mess dress and starched shirt, manifested at dinner to exchange small-talk; no children's hostess took the place of nanny. The age of the floating gin-palace had not yet come, nor had any slick bartender yet signed Articles to whisk his cocktail-shaker with the best of the smart set's favourite landbound barmen in London, New York and Paris. Throughout the nineteenth century the sea was a place of wet and hardship, and the emigrant run from Liverpool was, though comparatively short as compared with the voyage to Sydney Heads, among the hardest below decks.

The unfortunate traveller from poverty to Elysium had to pass through Hades first, and Hades began in Liverpool. First the would-be emigrants, fresh from the innocence of their hamlet, had to run the gauntlet of the conmen who largely formed the band of emigration agents and who, in return for cash, promised passages to the New World and boarding-house accommodation while waiting for the ship. The emigrants, especially the Irish, were exploited and plundered at every stage, sold passages that did not exist, piloted – sometimes by mates from the ships themselves it must be admitted – to rat-infested dwellings where they were charged exorbitantly for filthy straw mattresses in common lodging houses with little if any food provided. They were set upon by rival gangs of thieves, each anxious for the pickings; their baggage, such as it was, was snatched up at the docks and not released until a huge demand for carrying it had been met. Many parted with their carefully hoarded golden sovereigns for a give-away sum in dubious dollars, having been mendaciously informed by the money-changers that gold would not be allowed into North America. And it was not unknown for the Liverpool lodging house keepers, when they had found a good proposition to suck dry, to send a message across the Atlantic by the next fast ship to their friends in New York, giving the details of the luckless man's life, even to his parish, his relations, his priest and how much money he had left, so that on arrival he could be milked afresh, believing until it was too late that he had fallen among friends who knew his family.

Having survived the forty thieves of Liverpool, the emigrant, his passage wonderfully secured at last, would join the straggling human procession carrying its all below the warehouses at the berths, dodging the incoming and outgoing cargo slings – wool and grain from Australia, raw cotton, beef, mutton, bacon and hams; manufactured goods for export, iron and steel, wool and cotton made-up garments, machinery and mill work. Liverpool was becoming the earthworm of the seaborne trade, the vehicle that sucked in and spewed out again, aerating the world of commerce. If the emigrant survived the cargo slings he had yet to dodge the cordage: rope was everywhere, leading from bollards, through fairleads, over winches and underfoot – and any foolish landsman who put his interfering foot into a bight of it incurred shouts of abuse from busy mates, and possibly a stove-in head at the same time should the slack of the rope be taken up before his foot was out of it. Everywhere would be the sight and sound of movement – the derricks of the steamers lifting the slings with the steam-winches rattling and belching, the sailing ships hoisting in by pully-hauley, mates calling orders, rudery flowing back from the stevedores as they heaved at the cased goods with their shining and lethal cargo-hooks, terrible implements that from time to time, wielded in drink outside the public houses of Liverpool and other ports, tore out throats and eyes.

So when the passengers for the New World boarded their ship, they entered the same world of discipline as did the crew, with God and His deputy in firm control. Passengers did not demand; paying their fares, they obeyed at the same time. As an example of what was required of them, Her Majesty's Order in Council dated 6 October 1849 for 'Preserving Order and Securing Cleanliness and Ventilation on board Passenger Ships proceeding from the United Kingdom to any of Her Majesty's Possessions abroad' speaks eloquently. True, the United States was not a possession of the Queen of England by this time, but Canada at all events was, and the general principle held good, and in all ships engaged in the passenger trade the masters authenticated Her Majesty's commands by giving them the seal of their own approval.

Thus, the Rules for Passengers provided that all must rise at 7 am sharp, unless otherwise permitted by the surgeon, and that they were to be abed by 10 pm. No naked lights were allowed at any time or on any account. When dressed the Passengers – allowed by the Rules a capital P, curiously enough – were to roll up their bedding, sweep the decks, including the space under the bottom of the berths, and to throw the dirt overboard; breakfast was not to commence until this had been done. The sweepers for the day were to be taken in rotation from the males above the age of fourteen, and single women were to keep their own compartment clean. On Sundays the Passengers were to muster at 10 am, when they were expected to appear in clean and decent apparel, the day itself to be observed as religiously as circumstances might admit. No gunpowder was to be brought aboard, nor loose hay or straw allowed below. The Passengers had to bring their own food aboard, and cook it throughout the voyage, and on embarkation an officer checked that each person had his rations, utensils and cooking equipment.

The berthing arrangements were of the most primitive kind in most ships. The emigrant trade was to a large extent carried on by the timber ships, vessels that were sent across to bring back timber and would mostly have gone out in ballast had it not been for the easy availability of human freight. So the holds, which would be full of wood cargo homeward, were rigged as makeshift messdecks for the outward run, with tiered bunks set close together below the cargo hatches to accommodate as many people as possible. The result, in anything approaching a seaway, could be imagined; and all too often, the revolting combination of smells from so many close-packed unwashed bodies and from dirty clothing would add to its quota.

But none of this deterred the men and women who had seen the great luring light of the United States – Canada, it appears, was less popular, at any rate with the Irish, since by and large the Irish were disillusioned with anything British: the Union Flag was not liked any more, even though the British government tried to redeem it by offering to haul emigrants to Canada up the St Lawrence River in barges, to be provided free of charge. That is, if they ever got there: in 1846, 106,000 Irish and Scots emigrants crossed, or tried to cross, the North Atlantic; 12,200 died at sea or upon arrival, and 7,000 more joined them within a matter of weeks of landing. There were tragedies at sea, such as the fate of the 1300-ton ship *Ocean Monarch*, which left Liverpool for Boston in 1848 carrying 338 emigrants. Some of

The emigrants below deck lived in wretched conditions in congested quarters.

them started a fire in a ventilator as they went down the Mersey, with the misguided intention of boiling a kettle. The fire went out of their control and spread fast, soon beyond the capacity even of the crew, whose efforts were hampered by the panic that spread with the flames. Other ships in the vicinity came to the *Ocean Monarch*'s assistance but the ship sank in the bay with a death toll of 178. Eye-witness accounts said that the survivors, fleeing ahead of the fire as it took hold, moved forward until they were crowding the jib like ants, eventually bringing so much weight to it that when the burning foremast fell it parted the jib stays and the whole lot plunged into the sea, which was running very heavily.

In the previous year the ship *Exmouth*, out of Londonderry for Quebec, drove into a deep rock cleft on the island of Islay on Scotland's west coast. One hundred and eight bodies were recovered, most of them women and children, naked and mutilated, many headless and limbless. Between the years 1847 and 1853, a short enough span in all conscience, no less than fifty-nine emigrant ships were lost in

the North Atlantic trade, with a very heavy toll of life. Ill-equipped in many cases to carry and control such large numbers of passengers, they were frequently overcome by the sheer panic that resulted from some quite small mishap, so that a minor matter was turned into a disaster, and most of the blame for this must lie with the greed of certain of the owners, whose sole aim appears to have been to cash in while the easy availability was there, and never mind the risks – nor the rules and regulations either: they could be got around by clever and determined makers of profit.

Disease

Tragedy, however, did not come only by way of shipwreck: indeed, in spite of the number of losses, which in today's light seem scandalous and appalling but which were only to be expected in more adventurous and dangerous days, the lives swallowed by the sea's hazards were as nothing when compared with the losses by disease. At the best of times the nineteenth century was scarcely a bloomingly healthy one: in the horrible conditions of many of the emigrant ships, sickness flourished as nowhere else. In the great ship-fever year of 1847 all the New York quarantine hospitals were overwhelmed with the sick, and the City Almshouse with the destitute; at the quarantine station warehouses were pressed into service to accommodate the fever's overflow, and special buildings were put up on Staten Island. The United States were forced ultimately to refuse entry to vessels having fever aboard, which at one time, so prevalent was disease, meant that virtually every arriving ship was turned away, with terrible consequences as they beat back again to sea with their dead and dying and their supplies of food and water running out.

Many of these ships headed for the St Lawrence and a Canadian arrival instead, with the result that conditions at Grosse Island, the Canadian quarantine station in the St Lawrence River, became even more terrible than those in New York. There were at one time 2500 sick of the fever, and more coming in with every tide, existing in misery and filth, with little medical attention, and suffering the molestations of so-called nurses whose sole objective was the robbery of the dead. Grosse Island coped at different times with ship-fever, cholera and typhus, and contains something in the region of 11,000 bodies buried. On the island stands a monument bearing an inscription to the memory of the many thousands of persons 'who flying from Pestilence and Famine in Ireland in the year 1847 found in America but a Grave'.

Both at Grosse Island and in New York the scourge and horror of the sickness was widespread and appalling, but those at Grosse Island were possibly spared the ordeal of one Henry Lloyd, who arrived in New York in July 1851 and, being ill, requested hospitalization. He was placed in an overcrowded barrack on Ward's Island, a verminous bed was provided, and his complaint about the smell was met by a drunken doctor with the comment that if he didn't like it he should 'prevail upon the other men to contain their farting'.

By 1847 the flight from Ireland in particular had become a mass exodus, with the very roads to the ports blocked by would-be escapers from the terrible ravages of the potato famine. Chicanery in these conditions ran riot: ships sailing from the Irish ports gave not a fig for the load regulations (such as they were) or for passenger safety, leaving with false passenger rolls, with short water and rations, with virtually no sanitary facilities other than the accommodation holds themselves, with men and women, when the weather permitted, dangling their bottoms over the side from the shrouds to gain relief. The overcrowding was a danger to all aboard: in one ship 32 official berths were shared between 276 actual passengers, persons whose names appeared on no list anywhere. Even before this, in 1843, seventeen British ships had sunk inside the St Lawrence River alone, losing more than 700 lives. These were the coffin ships eventually cleared from the seas by Samuel Plimsoll, the British politician known as 'the sailors' friend', a Bristol-born London coal merchant who became Member of Parliament for Derby in 1868 and who was largely responsible for the passing of the Merchant Shipping Act of 1876, which empowered the Board of Trade to detain any vessel deemed unsafe and made compulsory on every ship the Plimsoll mark to indicate clearly its maximum load line.

By the middle of the century the American Passenger Acts made an attempt – easily and often circumvented by the profit-motivated dishonest on both sides – to discourage destitute emigrants from entering the country. This destitution had become an enormous problem, and the citizens of America were, understandably enough, fed up with the apparently unstemmable tide. Passenger fares were increased to make it harder for the poor to afford passage, while in Boston and New York it became permissible for the authorities to demand bonds from the ships' masters guaranteeing all their passengers against becoming a charge on their host country's taxpayers. This naturally made masters extremely hesitant to embark anybody with so much as a runny nose, a generally unhealthy look about him, or an air of having come down rather too far in the world. Inside America the rapidly increasing reaction against the new arrivals, with their diseases and grinding poverty, was directed chiefly against the long-suffering Irish. At the river and lake ports the ferryboat captains turned the hopeful Irish away from their vessels, leaving them stranded where they stood. It became a wonder that any shipping company was still willing to undertake the risk of the trade at all. Yet the answer was, as ever, to be found in the need to fill the outward-bound timber ships; nothing was less paying and more wasteful than a ship in ballast, occupying time and crew. Few cargoes went to North America outward in those years – the land was too thinly populated and its shopping-basket was a small one – but the timber ships had valuable freights to pick up, so had to get there.

Such was the emigration from and through Britain, and it is worth noting that in sharp contrast the ships arriving across the Atlantic with German and Polish emigrants from Hamburg and Bremen were well-found vessels bringing healthy cargoes of men and women and children, decently dressed, happy people who sang with vigour and hope as they first saw the shores of their new lands. Conditions in British ships and the health and quality of British emigrants were to improve out of all recognition by the end of the century, but by that time the passage of the Atlantic was being made by steam. As ever, steam brought less adventure; but it also brought greater comfort and less hazard, as well as a faster end to seasickness.

4

Race from the Orient

There was a tremendous feeling of romance about the China trade in the nineteenth century. The world was large in those days, China and the Far East more distant than now in terms of time taken to cover the sea miles, the long haul outwards a circuitous one, at any rate in the eyes of landlubbers – by way of the trade winds across almost to Brazil out of the English Channel, then southward through the Doldrums with the assistance, lethargic enough, of the Brazil Current. A long beat through the south-east trades of the South Atlantic into the north-west and west trades as far as the Cape of Good Hope, on across the southern part of the Indian Ocean to the East Indies, through the Sunda Strait towards the coast of Borneo with its head-hunters, and up past Singapore into the South China Sea between the Philippines and Cochin China.

The Chinese themselves were, at any rate in the early years, an unknown quantity, but what was told of them indicated that they were as tricky, as devious and as dangerous as their treacherous coasts. Piracy abounded in the China seas: ship after ship from the West was lured to its destruction, boarded and pillaged and its crew put to the sword. Even in the major trading ports of Shanghai, Canton and Foochow the pirates lurked in the approaches and the pilotage was, to say the least, unreliable. Many of the Chinese pilots were in league with the pirates themselves and, far from offering assistance and advice to shipmasters, sought only to pile up the vessels so that they could be conveniently stripped and plundered. As for the European pilots, when they were to be found, many proved to be more often drunk than sober, and even when in the latter state left a lot to be desired in their knowledge of the waters.

As always with the romantic vision, the reality behind it was hard work, hard sailing, and hard men. One of the great names of the China trade was that of Killick – Captain James Killick, who had started his apprenticeship in the brig *Ganges* in the Baltic trade in 1833, when he was sixteen years of age. At the age of twenty-nine he took command of the *John Dugdale* out of Liverpool, remaining in this ship for some five years. After twelve months ashore he took command of the famous clipper ship *Challenger*, built by Richard and Henry Green of Blackwall, a clipper whose genesis was due to a desire on the part of her British owners to beat the United States ship *Challenge*, a clipper of 2000 tons launched at New York on 24 May 1851.

Challenge was a real flyer, and in 1852 when lying ready for tea in China, gave rise to a stake of £10,000 – which was not taken up – offered by the American Navigation Club for a race between the American and British flags. *Challenge* was a large ship, her main truck being a little over 200 feet from the waterline, her main yard 90 feet long, and her full suit of canvas a towering picture in white. Both she and *Challenger* loaded for London, *Challenger* at Shanghai, *Challenge* at Canton, the former leaving for home on 28 July and the latter on 5 August. Although the

stake had been turned down, the two masters in fact embarked upon an unofficial race for the London River. *Challenge* passed Anjer Point into the Indian Ocean two days ahead of *Challenger*, and arrived at Gravesend on 19 November. Captain Killick in *Challenger* arrived in London on 17 November after a total passage of 112 days as against *Challenge*'s 106 but, since Shanghai is around 850 miles north of Canton, the passages were in fact about equal. Killick continued to command *Challenger* as the American onslaught on the tea trade gathered way. His last voyage ended in December 1860 and he swallowed the anchor (or, left the sea), but did not forsake the China scene: joining with one James Henry Martin he founded the shipbroking and shipowning firm of Killick, Martin and Company which, together with Jardine, Matheson, remained one of the most respected names on the China coast.

The China tea run was possibly the most glamorous of all the many aspects of the sailing ship days, but sadly it was also the shortest-lived. Its beginning was roughly coincidental with the repeal in 1849 of the Navigation Laws in Britain, Acts of Parliament that from about 1381 had protected British commerce, ships and seamen from foreign competition even to the extent that from 1660 no goods, with certain exceptions, might be imported into Britain or its dependencies except in British bottoms. These Acts led to severe and restrictive retaliation, which was removed by their repeal, and the heyday of the tea trade with China and the Far East began, continuing, so far as sail was concerned, until the mid-Eighties but, after the opening of the Suez Canal, on a much reduced scale. It was in fact the United States that started the ball really rolling when in 1850 the clipper *Oriental* berthed in London with tea from China. She became the

The *Gorch Fock*, a romantic view reminiscent of the golden age of sail.

The crew of the HMS *Challenger*.

awed objective, as it seemed, of every sightseer in the British capital as she lay in the West India Dock; she was at that time the biggest clipper to be seen in the Thames, and to add financial injury to insulted pride her tea fetched £6 a ton, just double the price for the cargoes from the British clippers.

Nevertheless, the British responded well: this was a trade that was to develop the best in British seafaring and shipbuilding and the finest of clippers began sailing the run east, taking out cargoes of Cardiff coal, coke, thread and yarn, and sundry items of general freight. Such names as *Lothair*, *Wylo*, *Kaisow*, *Ariel*, *Titania*, *Thermopylae*, *Spindrift* and *Leander* crop up through the racing years in the arrivals and departures lists between London and the far distant China coast. The competition to bring the cargoes back first to the London market was intense, and very personal to the masters and crews, and indeed to the builders as well. *Cutty Sark* herself owed her genesis to a determination to beat *Thermopylae*, launched a year earlier from Walter Hood's yard at Aberdeen and destined expressly for the China tea trade.

Captain John Willis Junior, son of the sailing ship master who had been the 'Old Stormy' immortalized in the sea chanty 'Stormalong', commissioned *Cutty Sark* from the Scots builder Hercules Linton and his new Clyde shipyard. John Willis Junior, known to seafarers and the City as 'Old White Hat' from his customary headgear, an impressive man with a full beard as white as the famous hat, had a burning ambition to win the annual race home from China with the first of the season's tea. Willis's standards for construction as laid down in the building contract were so high, and his bargaining so hard, that the unfortunate builders were driven into bankruptcy. Never before had they attempted anything so large as a clipper ship, and had been anxious for prestige purposes to secure the contract at any cost, but they were beaten by Willis's figure of £17 per ton. Thus *Cutty Sark* was completed by Denny Brothers, also on the Clyde. Launched by the wife of her first master, Captain Moodie, *Cutty Sark* went down the Clyde under tow for fitting out at Greenock, and sailed on her maiden run to Shanghai out of London on 16 February 1870; but it was not until 1872 that she and her rival *Thermopylae* met for a race on equal terms.

Thermopylae – smart and trim, with her green painted hull, white lower masts and yards, and with gold leaf in plenty – was already building up a formidable reputation as a sailer and racer. A composite-built ship of very beautiful lines, she was of much the same displacement and dimensions as *Cutty Sark*, and as much a favourite of her day, a notable ship that had broken records every voyage since her maiden run to Australia. On this run she had left Gravesend at 5 am on 7 November 1868, passing the Lizard at 6 pm next day and clearing the Channel the same night. She let go her anchor off Port Phillip, Melbourne, sixty days later pilot to pilot. From Melbourne she sailed for Newcastle, New South Wales, to

The tea clipper *Titania* in the Old Britannia dry dock in London.

load for Shanghai. Her passage of twenty-eight days from Newcastle to Shanghai set up another record, and from Shanghai to London in ninety-one days was yet another – though this, as it happened, was to be beaten within a fortnight by *Sir Lancelot*, owned by James MacCunn: she made the passage home from Foochow against the monsoon in eighty-four days.

Cutty Sark races Thermopylae
Before their great race, the *Cutty Sark* and *Thermopylae* loaded together at Shanghai, sailing from Woosung on the same day. There was keen competition between Captain Moodie of *Cutty Sark* and Captain Kemball of *Thermopylae*, and Moodie was determined to bring down the flaunting golden cock, a-crow from Kemball's masthead. Yet contemporary accounts indicate that in fact Moodie, though a competent and conscientious seaman, was not a driver, whilst Kemball had the reputation of being one of the best masters of the day and a man never afraid to crack on. This latter, together with an inbred knowledge, an intuition, of just how much sail a ship could take without carrying away sails, masts and yards in a tangle of smashed wood and parted rope, was the essential, vital quality required to win.

The start of the run can well be seen in the mind's eye: the tow down the Yangtse for the open sea beyond Woosung Island, a highly valuable cargo of tea under hatches, all bargaining over, freight rates settled, and hopes high in saloon and fo'c'sle aboard each ship for the winning of the £100 bonus plus ten shillings per ton of freight for the first cargo to reach the merchants of Mincing Lane. Down through the China seas, thrusting south, a little before the typhoon season was due, each ship within sight of the other – together they reached Anjer Point in the Sunda Strait and passed into the grey, monsoon-swept seas of the Indian Ocean, *Thermopylae* now one-and-a-half miles in the lead. Course was set through the heaving waters westwards for the Cape of Good Hope, leaving the island of Mauritius to starboard, with anchors lashed down on the fo'c'sle-head, cables unshackled and stowed and the hawse-pipes plugged. Driving into those cold grey seas, with water shipped over the bows to fling aft and wash around the marooned deckhouses before pouring in a foaming cascade back through the scupper vents, with all possible canvas set and straining out from the cringles as the ships raced for home, each master would have been on deck constantly, watching the helm, watching the sails, watching the wind and sea.

It was all up to the master's personal skill and judgment whether he should take a northerly or a southerly course towards the Cape, how he coaxed and cajoled and drove and bullied the ship along, whether he chose in the later stages to hug the coastlines close or stand well out to sea. Each small shift of wind must be anticipated before it came with its tearing gusts to rip canvas to flying shreds and smash great seventy-foot yards like matchwood. Below decks the conditions would have been bad: the seas had a nasty way of getting below, of soaking bedding and dousing such fires as might have been permitted in saloon and galley. Water would swill around the master's and the mates' cabins, and the water in the apprentices' berths amidships would very likely be deeper than was normal – but apprentices were considered to be used to this and dared not moan. There would be no chance, perhaps for weeks, of drying out, and hot food and drinks would be scarce if not totally unobtainable. No comfort anywhere, and only work, hard work in wind and wet and cold, right around the clock: though the deck watches were set alternately, four hours on and four hours off throughout the voyage, the call for 'All Hands' was liable to come at any moment and weary men just off watch would tumble out again from their sodden bunks and go aloft to the yards and footropes or strain their guts out on sheets and braces and halliards.

In the latter years of the nineteenth century, barques began to succeed the wooden clippers.

Gradually on this occasion *Cutty Sark* drew ahead, leaving *Thermopylae* to drop back until she was hull down, and then right out of sight astern. Twenty-six days out from the Sunda Strait and now off Algoa Bay some four hundred miles eastward of the Cape, *Cutty Sark* was nicely ahead and sailing well through very heavy weather with the crests of the waves blown in spindrift that gave all the appearance of a white carpet laid over the turbulence of the sea, when disaster hit her a savage blow: she suddenly found her rudder carried clear away from the gudgeons.

Such an accident at sea can mean tragedy: with all steering gone, a ship can broach-to in a trice, falling off to come broadside to the wind and sea to be smashed and pounded by gigantic waves dropping aboard in sound and fury to break deckhouse and hatch covers to splinters, to carry away lifeboats, to bring masts and yards down on unprotected heads. But on this occasion supreme seamanship on the part of Captain Moodie and his crew kept the vessel safe and on an even keel; work done above and beyond the call of duty by *Cutty Sark*'s carpenter, Henry Henderson, eventually restored her capacity to steer. Aboard *Cutty Sark* at the time happened to be her owner's brother, and he took it upon himself to give unwarrantable orders to Captain Moodie to make into Cape Town for repairs. Moodie had absolute confidence in Henry Henderson, and here indeed was a classic example of the master's sovereign authority even in the face of his owner's representative: Moodie refused pointblank to take such an order, even threatening to put Willis in irons and charge him with mutiny if he persisted, and instead gave Henderson the orders that led to the construction of the jury rudder. Henderson, a Scot from Kincardine, had been concerned all the way through in *Cutty Sark*'s construction, and knew the ship, timberwise, like the back of his horny hand. There could be no one better fitted to make a jury rudder. And this he did, working for six days in terrible weather on spare spars and iron stanchions, forging chain to be shackled to the new rudder and led to the ship's wheel through fairleads. Thanks to Henderson, tragedy did not occur, but the race was already lost. Even so, *Cutty Sark* reached the London River only a week behind *Thermopylae* and, had she not suffered the setback of the accident, might well have won.

Cutty Sark never did win the first-of-the-season tea race, but throughout her years as a China tea clipper she maintained the great traditions of sail under skilful, dedicated masters, men who could not afford to know the meaning of fear as they drove the ship through waters and currents and largely uncharted channels, to gain valuable hours over their rivals. In the case of *Cutty Sark*, her greatest glories were to come later, in the Australian wool trade. She never really shone as a tea clipper, and in fact made no more than eight tea voyages, carrying an average cargo of 1,325,000 lbs of tea in chests.

With just twenty minutes between them, the *Ariel* and the *Taeping* raced up the Thames to the East India dock.

The Greatest Tea Race of All

The most famous race of all, and the closest, was that between the composite ships *Ariel* and *Taeping*, each of them three-masted ship-rigged vessels. *Ariel*, of 853 tons net, from Robert Steele's yard at Greenock on the Clyde, black hulled with pink masts and yards, was commanded by Captain Keay. *Taeping*, with her superb finish, her gingerbread work and deck fittings of brass-inlaid teak, of 724 tons, also from Steele's yard, was commanded by Captain Dowdy.

Both ships left Foochow on 30 May 1866, sailing together on the same tide, with *Serica* a few minutes behind. *Ariel* had loaded her cased tea first, from 24 to 28 May, and had then been towed by a steam tug to a deepwater anchorage for the night. At 5 am next morning she was on her way down the river to the sea when her tug got into difficulties and collided with her. Once again she anchored, and her master suffered the fury of seeing another ship, *Fiery Cross*, go by as he lay stopped. A whole night was wasted, and when morning came there was another delay, this time due to rain and mist, and both *Taeping* and *Serica* were able to catch *Ariel* up on the 30th. Next day, 31 May, the race proper began, a battle of skill and determination and hardships through the China seas to Java in the teeth of strong winds, with 14,000 miles of deep water to cross from Foochow to the Channel pilot. At noon on 18 June *Ariel* and *Taeping* passed the signal station in the Sunda Strait five hours apart, *Ariel* leading. Coming out of the narrows into the Indian Ocean, they found the south-east trades blowing steady and strong, and all possible canvas was sent aloft to the yards. Farther south as they stormed along, both ships found good easterly winds, and *Ariel*, once around the Cape of Good Hope and into the South Atlantic half a day ahead of *Taeping*, was able to take a direct course towards St Helena, but once there was unlucky enough to meet only light winds. *Taeping*, whose master had held her nearer the African coast, found stronger winds and was able to make up the time lost earlier. *Taeping* sighted St Helena on 27 July and at Ascension Island was leading the race, though she and *Ariel* found themselves later neck-and-neck across the Equator.

Next came the Doldrums, the broad band of calm in which ships could lie still and silent upon the Ancient Mariner's 'painted ocean' for weeks on end, waiting to catch the smallest hint of wind to fill their sails – the second-best suit that was always sent aloft in the calms, since the constant slatting against the masts made for extreme wear and tear. That year the calms extended, as it happened, farther northward than usual. However, *Ariel* managed to find a puff or two, and got and retained a lead. On 20 August, though both ships passed Flores in the Azores within a matter of hours of each other, it was *Ariel* who was still leading. As they neared the home latitudes the weather freshened and the racing clippers met strong westerly and south-westerly gales, but soon after midnight on 5 September *Ariel* raised the Bishop Rock in the Scillies, with *Taeping* now out of sight astern.

Celebration, however, was premature: at daybreak *Taeping* was observed away to starboard, tearing along with all sail set. Together they came up the Channel at something like fourteen knots; past the Lizard, Start Point, Portland, the Needles – one ahead a little, then the other. Not until they were past the Isle of Wight did either take off any sail, and then only as a matter of necessity, so that there was space for the hands to clear away the anchors and shackle up the cables for entry to the London River and the berth.

Midnight: and both ships passed Beachy Head. Early next morning they were together off Dungeness, asking for pilots. As the pilot cutter approached, *Ariel's* master edged in so as to pick up his man first, and *Taeping* tried to pass her with the same objective in view, but *Ariel* swung round in an instant of highly skilled handling and blocked her way. At 6 am *Ariel* had her pilot aboard, and was away for the Downs, gaining a mile of sea before *Taeping* could follow. *Ariel* was still leading off Deal, where each ship took a steam tug to tow upriver.

Taeping was lucky, in so far as she obtained the services of a much more powerful tug than did *Ariel*, and on entering the Thames she went well ahead, leading *Ariel* by nearly an hour at Gravesend. Then *Taeping* had to anchor to await the tide, and up once more came *Ariel*. At 9 am next day *Ariel* was off the East India Dock, where she was to berth, but she had too much depth to be able to enter, and was forced to wait for the next tide. *Taeping*, meanwhile, proceeded ahead to the London Docks, and at 10 pm went straight in and got a rope ashore. Just twenty minutes too late to win, *Ariel* managed to do likewise. So close was the race that the masters agreed to share the prize money and the bonus. Of the other ships, *Serica* entered four hours later, to be followed next day by *Fiery Cross* and *Taitsing*. *Ariel* and *Taeping* had made the passage home in the splendid time of ninety-nine days out from the Min Kiang. Incredible skill and seamanship were necessary to bring five ships to port so close together when, through 14,000 miles of stormy sea and calm, they had seldom sighted one another – skill that is probably quite lost today.

It is not surprising that many shipmasters were persons of a quite extraordinary eccentricity, for the stresses and strains of such close races, lived out in the lonely isolation that was their lot – both by the fact of being at sea for many months at a stretch and because as masters they remained mostly aloof from the crew – was virtually bound to tend towards an idiosyncratic attitude towards their ships. The *Wylo*, one of the greatest of the tea clippers, built by Robert Steele and owned by Killick, Martin, suffered an accident to her third mate while on passage from London to Shanghai in 1876. In the south-east trades this officer was working aloft on the mizzen topgallantyard when he lost his foothold and fell some 100 feet to the deck, breaking two ratlines, hitting the gunwale of the lifeboat, and taking the deck with his head, very hard. Miraculously he was not severely damaged, but the soft pine of the deck planking suffered a deplorable dent. The master, Captain W.H. Browne, was displeased and, so the story goes, before attending to the third mate sent for the carpenter, who was ordered to employ a hammer to smooth out the dented deck. One does not wish to generalize about a fine body of seamen, but it is true to say that in at least some cases the stark loneliness of command at sea led in one of two directions, the Bible or the bottle, God or alcohol, and sometimes both: many was the first mate driven to distraction by repeated saloon readings of who begat whom, and what happened in Sodom and Gomorrah.

Opium

Tea was not the only commodity for which the great sailing ships traded to the Far East. The running of opium, mainly from India to China, was both important and lucrative, and this trade extended from Bombay to Korea, from Calcutta to Japan, from Moulmein to Manila: the Indian Ocean and the waters around Java were as closely involved as were the China seas. In the early days it was a curiously-based trade, half above-board and half not; there was no official ban, and though all kinds of difficulties had been placed in its way, even Warren Hastings, Governor of Bengal, had sent a cargo of opium to China in 1781. But in the year 1800 all sale of the drug had been forbidden in China, and as so often happens this served only to increase the total of imports. In the previous year, 1799, a formal edict had been issued making opium contraband, and a second such edict was issued in 1809. Notwithstanding this, the American brig *Sylph* arrived in 1811 in the Canton River with the first cargo of Turkish opium from Smyrna, and in 1817 the great East Indiaman *Vansittart* arrived with the Turkish product. During

left Hong Kong in the days of sail.

below Landing goods at Calcutta.

that year over a thousand chests of opium were imported by Portuguese ships into Macao. The prices at the East India Company's Calcutta sales soon soared sky-high, and in 1819 an opium mart was opened in Bombay. The British brig *Mentor* was said to be acting as an opium 'godown' at Whampoa, thus becoming the first opium-receiving ship on the China coast. In the following year the anchorage off Lintin established a reputation as a rendezvous for outside shipping, and became a haunt of opium smugglers.

The first of the British opium clippers was *Red Rover*, launched into the Hooghly by the Howrah Dock Company on 12 December 1829. She was owned by Captain Clifton, formerly of the Royal Navy and the East India Company's ships. Sold later to Jardine, Matheson, she remained in their service until she was lost in the early Seventies. Another was *Falcon* which, after loading tea for London in the autumn of 1837, was shifted to the opium trade. There was a need for fast ships to carry not only opium but silks between Canton and Bombay and Calcutta, and a number of the schooner fliers such as *Hellas* and *Time* were diverted to this traffic. In her opium days *Hellas* carried a crew of fifty men, and was heavily armed. *Time* was provided with a brass 12-pounder pivot gun placed amidships, and six 4-pounders.

There was a great sense of adventure about the life on the China coast, where the masters had not only to deal with typhoons and attacks by pirate *prahus* but also, when engaged in the opium trade, make business deals with wily Indians and Chinese and with the dodgy traders of Malaya. By 1821 the smuggling into the Pearl River had reached immense proportions, and was carried on almost openly, much chicanery and double-talk being indulged in by the mandarin representatives of the Son of Heaven, or Emperor of China, as they angled for their Emperor-proof whack of *cumshaw*. Each season there were more and more European and Parsee merchants appearing at Canton and Macao, most of them hiding their semi-nefarious trade under the cloaking but phoney consular flag of some unlikely state such as Prussia, Sardinia or even Galilee. Canton presented a colourful picture with its ragged-trousered fortune-tellers, its vociferous quacks selling their wondrous panaceas to cure everything from headache to syphilis, the money-changers, the gaping crowds of loiterers in the square between the thirteen foreign 'authorized' factories and the Pearl River. There were all kinds of trades being carried on from the clustered booths: barbers cutting hair in the open, desiccated old women selling needles and thread, fruit sellers, cobblers, purveyors of livestock and vendors of flesh whose goods negated the efforts of the patent-medicine sellers. At the eastern end of the square lay the Creek, filled with sampans and their many boat-dwelling families – a muddy, stinking ditch at low water with, at its far side, the *hongs* or warehouses of the Chinese merchants. Canton was a sailor's town as well as an opium town, an Oriental Liverpool.

opposite Four masters in the Hughli.

At sea the percentage of ship casualties in the opium trade was very high: many of the clippers vanished without trace, as many as one third of all the ships engaged falling victim either to pirates or the weather and navigational hazards. Islands, reefs, sandbanks, currents that changed with the speed of quicksilver – all these had to be negotiated. The stately East Indiamen kept their sailings to the fair-weather·times, and kept themselves clear of such dangers as the Paracel and Pratas Reefs, and the archipelago of rocks and shoals westward of the Palawan Passage, but things were different for the clippers. Their prime object was to get the opium into the Chinese market from India twice or three times a year and that meant keeping the seas in all weathers and through all dangers, and cutting the corners on all possible occasions. This involved a steady hard slog to windward when working up from Singapore against the north-east monsoon, and strong currents had to be circumvented by tricky pilotage along uncharted coasts. When the wind blew light, any land or sea breezes had to be sought along the coasts of Borneo and Cochin China, the masters often standing brazenly into shoaling water with only inches beneath their moving keels, watchful for the junks that might come alongside with their sword-slashing, money-hungry crews.

The opium trade produced virtually the first trading craft with clipper lines, and in their turn these tall-masted, long-sparred ships produced an incomparable race of seamen and, indeed, the principal means whereby China and Japan were opened up to world trade. In 1839 there took place the so-called Opium War, which led to the opening up by Britain of the ports of Shanghai, Ning-po, Foochow and Amoy, besides Canton – and thus, indirectly, to the establishment of the tea trade itself, very largely for American owners at the start: until the repeal of the Navigation Acts no US ship could bring tea into the United Kingdom, but as soon as repeal came the Americans were in with a bang, and it is said that the opium ships acted as fine training craft for the masters and crews of the tea clippers.

By the end of the Fifties, the opium clippers on the Bombay and Calcutta runs were giving way to steamers such as Jardine, Matheson's *Reiver*, 778 tons, 400 horsepower, *Clan Alpine*, *Glengyle* and *Glenartney*. By this time also the Hong Kong Legislative Council had passed its Ordinance against Piracy, and from then on British warships made real attempts to stamp out the ravening fleets of *pilongs* along the China coast. Change had come with a semblance of law and order. The coast was never to be quite the same again.

The East Indiamen
The great British East Indiamen of the turn of the century were fighting ships as well as traders – big ships, well gunned, carrying silks, spices, tea, perfumes,

carpets, precious stones and what-have-you. In their heyday of glory they used to fight as men-o'-war, carrying naval gunnery rates and great broadsides that fired like Nelson's ships, the largest of them being equipped with forty to fifty heavy cannon to protect their immensely valuable cargoes from the pirates. On 14 February 1804 a homeward-bound fleet of East Indiamen, led by Captain Nathaniel Dance aboard the flagship *Earl Campden*, encountered a strong squadron of French ships – the 74-gun *Marengo* with the frigates *Belle Poule*, *Sémillante* and *Berceau*. Such a hurricane of fire from *Earl Campden*, *Royal George* and *Ganges* met the French that they turned tail and ran, and were under ignominious pursuit for two hours.

The captains of the East Indiamen were a race apart, the elite of the seafaring world. They were often immensely rich, owing to their privilege of shipping out fifty tons of their own goods for trade and barter and bringing back twenty tons of expensive freight from the East. Often they made up to £10,000 a voyage in this

Opening the Suez Canal eased passage to the East; here, the traffic of ships at Port Said.

way. In 1808 the Company owned fifty-four ships totalling 45,000-odd tons sailing on their trading voyages from Britain to India and China. Their *Essex* was the biggest sail carrier ever built, with sixty-three sails, twenty-one on the mainmast alone, and one side painted differently from the other to give her camouflage; at sea she was said to resemble a floating pyramid. But after 1833 the great 'John Company' that ruled the continent until the Mutiny in the Fifties was forbidden to operate ships at all other than strictly on the coast. Nevertheless their value echoed down the years ahead: the Company's sea officers had a great deal of experience in transporting large bodies of troops across the seas, and this knowledge was transmitted with benefit to the packet and emigrant ships as these emerged on the North Atlantic and Australian runs, the passenger trade being at that time an entirely new business for the owners, crews and builders.

Blackwall Frigates
The East Indiamen were replaced by a new breed, the well-found Blackwall frigates such as *La Hogue*, built at Sunderland in 1855 – 1330 tons, 226 feet in length, with a beam of 35 feet. She sailed regularly to Calcutta, but at the start of the Australian gold rush she began sailing to Melbourne and Sydney. She ended her life as a coal hulk at Madeira, being broken up in 1897. The Blackwall frigates were full-rigged vessels with painted ports, large figureheads and heavy sterns with quarter galleries, distinctively large fo'c'sles and long poops, and had several cabins for passengers. Four boats were normally carried at the davits, with two more in cradles on top of the deckhouse. They were not clippers, but they reduced the time taken to India from six to three months, and a round trip to China from two years to one.

Most of the Blackwall frigates were, as their name implies, built at Blackwall, on the Thames, and for a variety of owners, largely the firm of R. and H. Green of London. A curious story is told of one of them, the *Madagascar*, Blackwall-built for Green in 1837: in 1853 she vanished when crossing the Atlantic with passengers and gold, her end being one of those mysteries of the sea. Many years later a dying woman in New Zealand informed those at her bedside that on the *Madagascar*'s last voyage she had been a nurse on board, that there had been a mutiny, and that the officers had all been murdered. The passengers, taken prisoner, had been burned in a fire started by the mutineers – all except for the younger women, who had been rescued along with the gold cargo. Only two mutineers, and the woman now dying, had survived the surf, in which all the gold had also been lost forever. Subsequently one of the two surviving mutineers was hanged in San Francisco, while the other vanished like the *Madagascar* herself. It is a story that leaves many threads hanging, and in fact there was never any proof that the dying woman had spoken the truth.

opposite A procession of steam ships passes through El Kantara within a year of the opening of the Suez Canal.

Opposite
Above The USSR *Kruzenshtern* was
originally the *Padua*, built in
Germany for the Chilean nitrate run;
it is now used to train officers and
men of the USSR fishery fleet.
Below Recognizing the character-
building importance of training under
sail, almost every country in the
world now maintains a tall ship, often
for professional training, but
sometimes for youngsters who will
not make a career of the sea.

Opposite overleaf The beauty of the late
clippers is obvious in the intricate
rigging and billowing sails of the
Polish *Dar Pomorza*.

The Suez Canal Opens

Gradually the steamers were improving their performance, and with that the
end of the China clippers was in sight. In November 1869 the Suez Canal had been
opened, thus making available to steamers the short sea-route by way of the
Mediterranean, while the sailing ships had still to make the passage out and home
around the Cape of Good Hope, using their old allies the trade winds. Although
they could beat the early steamships on the Cape run, they could not do so when
those steamers were given their short cut, and sailing freights fell so far and so
rapidly that the trade was no longer viable.

By 1880 it was more and more difficult for any clipper to find a cargo at a
profitable figure, and in fact at certain times of the year few ships, either sail or
steam, were outward-bound for the Far East. Ships were down to tramping,
picking up cargoes where they could find them, with longer and longer voyages
away from their home ports. The *Kaisow*, a 795-ton tea clipper built in 1869 by Steele
at Greenock, leaving London for Hong Kong in April 1877, made her passage out
with general cargo and Cardiff coal in ninety-six days, then waited in vain for a
cargo homeward. Hong Kong produced nothing whatever, and the *Kaisow* sailed
for Portland, Oregon, three other ships leaving at the same time. On 15 September
Kaisow left Portland for China with another general cargo, crossing back to reach
Vancouver's Burrard Inlet fifty-one days later, this being the first of three
voyages she made across the Pacific, each time taking out a cargo of lumber from
Canada – a sad end for a proud tea clipper. And so it was that, with such steam
runs as the *Stirling Castle*'s twenty-nine days from Woosung to London *around the
Cape of Good Hope* in 1883, sail on the China run finally gave way to steam, and the
days of romance were over.

In *The Colonial Clippers* Basil Lubbock, that great chronicler of the age of sail,
writes:

> As o'er the moon, fast fly the amber veils,
> For one dear hour let's fling the knots behind,
> And hear again, thro' cordage and thro' sails,
> The vigour of the voices of the wind.
> They're gone, the Clyde-built darlings, like a dream,
> Regrets are vain, and sighs shall not avail,
> Yet, mid the clatter and the rush of steam,
> How strangely memory veers again to sail!

5

The Australian Route

WHEN speaking of the long run to the great Southlands of Australia and New Zealand, one thinks primarily of convicts, gold, and wool: and the convicts came first. They began going out on their harsh sentences of transportation to the colonies of the Australian continent in 1787, and there was no thought in the mind of authority that they might found an empire; they were sent out purely and simply because the home gaols and prison hulks were overcrowded and it had become vital that an alternative be found. And so in that year of 1787 the first fleet of convict vessels sailed for Port Jackson, the harbour of what was to become the great city and seaport of Sydney in New South Wales. The fleet, under Captain Arthur Phillip, Royal Navy, consisted of six convict transports containing more than 700 transportees, some two hundred of them being women, plus officers and marines and numerous civil officials with wives and families; there were also three store-ships, and the convoy was guarded by two men-o'-war. The conditions aboard the convict ships were grim in the extreme, but these conditions were very nearly equalled by the straightforward emigrant ships that by 1840 outnumbered the arrivals of the convict transports. A movement against transportation had grown up in Britain by this time: in 1840 it was forbidden by an Order in Council except to Van Diemen's Land and Norfolk Island, and in 1852 the last convict ship sailed from Britain.

Over the years since 1787, some 137,000 convicts had been landed in Australia, but this number was being overtaken by the arrival of ordinary emigrants from Britain who wished to make decent lives for themselves and were prepared to undergo the ordeal of the voyage out under sail. Broadly, the conditions aboard the emigrant ships were similar to those endured by the travellers to North America. The difference was that the New Australians had to endure them for a good deal longer. The voyage out via the Cape of Good Hope took an average of four months, with the ships running their easting down the high south latitudes from the Cape to the Leeuwin in cold and wet, with strong winds blowing around the world behind them or coming up, when they reached the Great Australian Bight, direct from the southern ice.

Imagination running riot could not present a worse picture than the facts of those emigrant voyages: the 'tween-decks were like dungeons, dark and hot at times, dark and cold at others, and almost always wet. The straw beds rotted with the constant ingress of seawater; the passengers, many of them sick and all of them dispirited and weakened by prolonged poor feeding, could all too often not stir themselves to go on deck to perform their natural functions, preferring to remain *in situ* for the purpose. The result was a fearful emanation of steam and stench whenever the hatches were opened up above their suffering heads: contemporary accounts speak of the smell being worse than that from a pigsty, and in this smell the passengers were forced to live and eat. As in the North

Atlantic trade, each passenger was responsible for cooking his or her own food, and this had to be done on deck if weather permitted. If the weather did not permit, or if the passengers were too ill to cope, the result was starvation. Frequently it was a case of the survival of the fittest: the strong did not always succour the weak, and in fact a large number of women in particular died on board from starvation. Those that survived starvation faced disease. When the ships called at the Cape, men and women so long cooped up in filthy conditions easily contracted infectious fevers, and the deaths on passage were many, the 'tween-decks often being sealed off to contain the spread, with the result that the sick were left to die and rot without help or medical attention.

The Gold Rush

As ever, human greed was the motivating force behind many an emigrant family's voyage of horror, and not for the first time in the history of the nineteenth century, gold was the focus of the greed. News reaching Britain in 1851 of the discovery of gold in Australia sent no less than 340,000 emigrants to take ship out of the port of Liverpool in search of the jackpot. The result may be imagined: the colonial trade took off like a rocket, all at once becoming the most vital in all the world. Gold fever, a disease as infectious as any other, drew men and women, English, Scots and Irish peasants who had never seen a ship in their lives in the majority of cases, to the ports and the high seas south. It was a fantastic business, and the Australian arrivals produced astonishing scenes. In Melbourne miners would descend aboard the ships, probably drunk, scattering gold dust to prove the word of the lucky strike, taking off their bush hats to show their fat rolls of bank notes stowed in the crowns. The crews deserted the ships in gold-mad legions, even the great Blackwallers losing their men. Guns and belaying-pins had to be used freely to prevent a total stampede. At one stage no less than fifty ships were laid up abandoned in Hobson's Bay: it was as bad as the earlier scenes at San Francisco. To get ships home it was necessary even to scour the gaols for crews, the fortunate ex-prisoners being paid £30 down and £3 a month for the passage. When the ships had crew enough to sail on the homeward run, the officers were forced to remain aft and armed to the teeth, permitting no member of the crew other than the man at the wheel to climb to the poop.

The first ship to land Australian gold in Britain was the Aberdeen White Star Line's *Phoenician*, which arrived off Plymouth on 3 February 1852 after an eighty-three-day run from Sydney under Captain Sproat, who established a record for the homeward voyage. She brought gold to the value of £81,000. The first ship to enter Liverpool with gold was the Eagle Line's packet *Albatross*, under Captain Gieves. She arrived at the end of August of the same year with £50,000 of gold dust

– and, miraculously, with precisely the same crew with which she had sailed from England initially.

So great was the rush to Australia that the Emigration Commissioners and owners found themselves sadly short of tonnage. In London the Blackwall frigates of Green, Money, Wigram and Smith – a merchant frigate, as opposed to a naval one, being defined as one that had a drop of four to five steps from poop to waist – were diverted from the splendour and riches of the Indian trade in a small attempt to cope with the rush. In Liverpool, owners began hiring or buying American transatlantic packets and clippers and ordered more tonnage from the

A view of the quayside and railway yard from Customs House in Newcastle, Australia, in the nineteenth century.

Boston and Nova Scotian yards. It became a common sight to see a dozen or more ships waiting for pilots inside Port Phillip Heads at the approaches to Melbourne. In 1852 the state of Victoria received 102,000 gold seekers; in the eighteen months following the gold strike Melbourne's population sped from 23,000 to 70,000 and Geelong's from 8,000 to 20,000. In the years 1852–7 Port Phillip took 100,000 English, 60,000 Irish, 50,000 Scots, 4,000 Welsh, 8,000 Germans, 3,000 Americans, a mere 1,500 French, and 25,000 Chinese, plus a variety of other but less proliferating nationalities.

Everyone was in an immense hurry to get at the gold, each convinced that wealth was his for the digging. This hurry, allied to economy, was the reason for the ship orders going across the Atlantic. It was well recognized that no other ships could match the Down Easters for sheer speed, and the outward-bound

Tall ships sometimes had to wait weeks to load the grain which came in sack by sack; but once underway, they maintained top speed to reach home ports with their cargo.

passengers always opted for the ships with the best reputations, the fast runners. Thus the Australian gold rush filled the shipyards of the United States with orders for large-capacity, passenger-carrying clippers. Even the route out changed in the vital interest of speed. Before the gold strike, vessels customarily followed the Admiralty route: they kept as much to the eastward as possible on their run south in order to avoid the dangers of Cape San Roque and its leeward currents; they then rounded the Cape of Good Hope close, indeed often called there, then kept well north of the forties when running their easting down. A passage of 120 days was thought very good; and when Captain Godfrey in the *Constance* went out in seventy-seven days by sailing a Great Circle track, he created something of a sensation in shipping circles.

Matthew F. Maury, an officer of the United States Navy, known as 'Pathfinder of the Seas' on account of his expertise in regard to winds and currents, dispelled the fears about Cape San Roque, showing that it could have little real effect on the fast ships coming along in the Fifties. He also demonstrated the advantage of sailing on a Great Circle, or meridian circle, from Cape San Roque in order to get as soon as possible into the high latitudes; he was opposed to the idea of bracing sharp up against the south-east trade-winds. His advice to Australia-bounders was to cross the equator in the vicinity of 30 degrees west and to run down through the south-east trades with topmast stuns'ls set, aiming to cross latitude 25 or 30 degrees south as the winds might permit, thence shaping a course more and more easterly until longitude 20 degrees east was crossed around latitude 45 degrees south. After reaching a maximum of 55 degrees south they were advised to haul up to the north as they approached Van Diemen's Land. By this new sailing method several fast passages were made, though only very well-found, powerful ships could in fact risk going far down into the high south latitudes. Captain Brown in *Runnymede* made Port Adelaide out of Liverpool in seventy-two days in 1852; and Captain Downward in *Anna* made the reverse run in the same year in seventy-six days, both ships being under 1000 tons. The English clippers *James Baines* and *Marco Polo* sailed the run from Liverpool to Geelong and Melbourne, and their stout oak and copper sheathing in fact proved to be stronger if heavier than the softwood American-built ships, which found it necessary to shorten sail in heavy weather sooner than oak-built ships, in order to avoid overstraining. The ships of the Black Ball and White Star Lines shipped emigrants out in such runs as seventy-five days, and James Baines, owner of the Black Ball Line, made his fortune from the great exodus to Australia.

The years of the gold rush resulted in a belated improvement in the standard of victualling and accommodation aboard the ships, beginning in fact to set the scale for the fine liners of later days. In 1853, aboard the emigrant ship *Eagle*, passengers were divided into four principal classes: cabin, saloon or deckhouse, second cabin, and intermediate or third class, which latter were again subdivided into 'enclosed' and 'open' berths. There were few double berths for families in the lowest class, and the sexes were split either side-by-side or fore-and-aft of the ship. All in all the rules were similar to those for the Atlantic run, with clear bedtimes indicated – lights out, no noise, up at 6 o'clock in the morning, no nonsense or be heaved from the bunk by the surgeon, who might well envy the more professional duties performed by his successors in present-day liners. The bunks themselves were divided one from another by plank partitions. Lavatory facilities were provided for women, but men had still to brave the upper deck and the wind and sea. Women also had the privilege of sick-berth accommodation in the stern. Water was at all times carefully watched, and two days were set apart in each week for the washing of clothes. If the would-be launderers had not saved enough fresh or rain-collected water, then the clothes had to be washed in salt water. Fresh or salt, it was always cold, and clothing was dried by being triced up in the rigging. If any passenger wanted wine or spirits he had to obtain a special dispensation from the captain, but the 'tween-deck passengers, the lowly mob, could buy ale and porter daily from 10 am to noon.

Liverpool, much more than London, became the kick-off point for the gold seekers. 'Liverpool on her stern and bound to go' became a watchword. Many ships were hired by the Government Emigration Department, but these were a mere fraction of the vessels on the Australian run. James Baines's Black Ball Line was joined by Pilkington and Wilson's White Star Line; by Henry Fox of Fox Line; Miller and Thompson of the Golden Line; Fernie Brothers of the Red Cross Line. Black Ball and White Star had the all-important mail contracts: James Baines accepted a contract to land the mails in sixty-five days, with a penalty clause of £100 a day for every day over. The famous *Marco Polo*'s first voyage to Australia was under charter to the Government Emigration Department; with 930 emigrants aboard and two doctors, she sustained only two adult deaths – a record in itself – and only a few children dead of the measles. At this time it was normal for ships carrying half *Marco Polo*'s passenger list to arrive in Hobson's Bay with fifty to a hundred deaths. *Marco Polo*, taking part in the renewed rivalry between the Black Ball and White Star Lines, was commanded by Captain Bully Forbes, a tough and ingenious man whose ideas of command were entirely original and who appeased the god of speed on one voyage by circumnavigating the globe via Cape Horn in 5 months 21 days.

Of Bully Forbes it was said that, when a deputation of passengers, scared of the way in which he was carrying sail, waited upon him cap in hand and begged him to shorten sail, he replied with a resounding 'No', adding that it was to be a case of Hell or Melbourne. He was said to padlock his sheets, not the bed variety but the rope one, and threaten his terrified crew with a revolver levelled from the poop and his eagle eye behind it, watching everything. Once, in response to a challenge, he crawled hand over hand from the spanker boom to the shark's fin on the jibboom; and when commanding *Lightning* he used to go out on the swinging boom when the lower stuns'l was set, and watch his ship from the boom end when she was roaring along before the westerlies, a highly dangerous proceeding. This curious action showed great trust in the man at the wheel, for if the ship had been brought a point or two nearer the wind, the end would have come speedily for Captain Forbes. But it was due to no such antics that the end came for the *Marco Polo*: in 1883 she piled up on Prince Edward Island and with her went a page of history. She was one more wreck in a sad list that had included such fine ships as *Young Australia*, *Champion of the Seas*, *Southern Empire*, *Royal Dane*, *Morning Star*, *Queen of the Colonies*, *Legion of Honour*.

Other great ships were sold to other flags: times were changing fast. Although with the United States torn by civil war in the 1860s the supremacy in overseas clipper trading had passed to Britain, it was a short-lived thing for the passenger-carrying sailing ships. By 1856 the struggle against steam had already become severe: in 1854 the iron full-rigged ship *Argo* of 1850 tons made use of her auxiliary engines to run from London to Melbourne in sixty-four days, and back around

The Australia-run clipper *Argo* at Melbourne, April 1891.

the Horn in sixty-three – the first merchant ship to circumnavigate the world by using steam power. This opened the floodgates; two years later the great P. & O. Line was on the scene to threaten the sailing-ship owners in the Australia passenger trade. And so vanished those ships, but in their eclipse were the already sprouting seeds of the wool clippers. As gold fever lost its heady temperature, as the emigrants became assimilated into the ways of their new land and began producing wool, hides, tallow, wheat and so on, a new kind of carrier was needed, and this meant new building. The emigrant ships out of Liverpool were unsuited to the new cargo trade – too big, too uneconomic, the repair bills too large for the softwood American-built clippers that grew water-soaked and strained over the years. So they dropped out, to be replaced by British-built hardwood ships of smaller tonnage, largely of teak, so that the repair bills were much less. These ships sailed the seas faithfully until they in their turn were replaced by the iron sailing ships from Aberdeen, the Clyde and Liverpool.

The Wool Trade
With the emergence of the wool clippers came the great, romantic races home, each master anxious to be first with a cargo for the London wool sales which took place between January and March of each year. It was the China tea trade all over again, with one exception: the fastest ship was loaded last, thus being given pride

Possibly loading up for another wool run, the *Cutty Sark*, *Brilliant* and *Yallaroi* at Sydney.

of place – that of last ship to leave, carrying many hopes of overhauling those slower ones that had left earlier. In the Eighties this pride of place was always accorded Old White Hat Willis's clipper *Cutty Sark*, commanded from 1885 by Captain Richard Woodget – a real driver, a firm man who pushed both ship and crew to the limit. Woodget was a splendid seaman and a fine leader, a captain to whom the crew gladly gave their best. Every year from 1885 to 1895 *Cutty Sark* beat the wool record, on each occasion beating her old China rival *Thermopylae*. The aim of every master on the run was to be reported as soon as possible after reaching soundings in the Channel, since the first sale lists were closed as soon as a sufficient number of cargoes had been reported actually arrived or coming up channel for the London River; and ships making their signal letters by noon on the opening day were included in those first sale lists. Should the master miss the sales, his cargo would have to be warehoused for perhaps two or three months until the next sales, and this obviously involved much additional expense to the owners for warehouse charges and loss of interest – not to mention the chances of a fall in the price of wool in the meantime.

A typical cargo would have included 3,550 bales of wool, 14,000 hides, 80 casks of tallow, 20 tons spelter, 4,000 ounces gold: such was the manifest of the ship *Omar Pasha*, Captain Thomas Henry, owned by G. Thompson, Sons and Company of Aberdeen, homeward bound from Melbourne in 1864. This ship also carried twelve passengers; and it is interesting to note pre-inflationary port charges of one shilling per ton, plus pilotage in and out at £28 18s 6d a time (As far back as 1947, the Suez Canal dues for the Orient Liner *Orion*, 24,000 tons, were around £10,000).

Wool was not an easy cargo to carry: the bales had to be 'screwed down' into the holds, and a good master would see to it that a ship was screwed down very hard indeed for maximum capacity, jammed to the limit with the bales; so tight did some masters cram their ships that wood and composite vessels used to have their decks and topsides specially caulked before loading wool. It was a very individual thing, all depending on the master: Captain Woodget used to cram 1000 more bales into *Cutty Sark* than his predecessor's best achievement, and made a point of being in the hold himself, in person, to supervise the screwing down. Wool is a spontaneously combustible cargo, and fire from dampened bales was responsible for the loss of many fine ships, such as *Fiery Star* and *Aurora*. The first mates of the wool clippers needed to keep an eagle eye on their cargoes, to spot at once any wisps of smoke from the hatches. Nothing burns faster than a ship at sea, and never mind the water with which she is surrounded: the enemy is the natural bellows borne by the wind.

One of the great flags of the Australian trade was still carried from the old emigrant days, flying bravely into the wool era – Aberdeen White Star, all of

The reflections of the masts of the
Clan Galbraith are so still she could be
in the Doldrums.

whose ships were built by Walter Hood of Aberdeen, real flyers, always clean and
well kept, outstanding for their smartness, painted green and with a gilt streak
along their sides, with figureheads, masts, spars and blocks painted white, decks
scrubbed as white, and all ropes' ends decently cheesed down – ships that were
on occasions sent up to China for a tea cargo home. On their outward passages to
Melbourne and Sydney they generally carried a few first-class passengers, though
it was only back in the gold rush days that their 'tween-decks were given over to
live freight. Aberdeen White Star's ships included *Phoenician*, *John Bunyan*, *Maid of
Judah*, *Queen of Nations*, and *Ethiopian*. The latter made her first voyage to Melbourne
in sixty-eight days under Captain William Edward, sailing her last voyage under
the British flag in 1886, being by that time reduced to barque rig. On her passage
home from Sydney she had a remarkable race with the iron ship *Orontes*. The two
vessels cast off their tugs together outside Sydney Heads, proceeded to sea and
next sighted each other off the Horn, afterwards being becalmed together in the
Doldrums, that listless area where masters were wont to whistle up the wind
while the sails flapped idly against the masts, then both spoke the same ship
(exchanged signals) off the Azores or Western Isles. As they reached the Channel,
Orontes came up under the counter of *Ethiopian*, which was hove-to taking
soundings in fog. Finally *Ethiopian* made the East India Docks one tide ahead of
Orontes, thus winning the race and a considerable sum in wagers. Subsequently
Ethiopian was sold to owners in Norway. In October 1894, bound from St Thomas to
Cork, she was abandoned off the Western Isles, afterwards being picked up derelict
some fifteen miles off Fayal, taken in tow for St Michael, and condemned.

Aberdeen was closely involved in the Australian trade: one of the best-known
firms, Duthie, built as well as owned wool clippers, and had timber interests as
well, maintaining some vessels in the North American timber trade. Indeed
Duthie's net was wide: they were among the first owners to send ships to the
Chinchas and Peru for guano. Their ships included the *Jane Pirie* of 427 tons,
Brilliant of 555 tons, *James Booth*, 636 tons, and *Ballarat*, 713 tons, the latter coming
home from Melbourne in a sixty-nine-day passage in 1855. In the previous year the
firm had built a wooden wool clipper, the *John Duthie*, of 1031 tons, following this
with another, the 1159-ton *Alexander Duthie*. In 1869 they produced the *Windsor Castle*
for Donaldson, Rose and Company, a ship that made many fine passages under
Captain Fernie, the best-known of her masters. Like so many other fine clippers,
Windsor Castle ended her days in the ignominy of coal hulkdom.

A good deal of the wool trade was carried on from the port of Adelaide in
South Australia, which state had from the early Fifties been sending home wool
cargoes in exchange for general goods out of London. This reciprocal trade had
been in the hands of the Orient Line, Devitt and Moore, and Elder, all of them
efficient, well-run companies. They sailed beautiful little composite-built ships,

overleaf No ship, whatever its construction, was ever free of the possibility of wreckage. The wrecked *Hansey* spills her timber cargo over the rocks of the Lizard in November 1911.

left The main centre of the Australian wool trade was Port Adelaide, here photographed in 1888.

most of them under 1000 tons and driven as hard as any Black Ball or White Star vessel. Although they never received the publicity or acclaim accorded the better-known lines, their masters were jealous enough of their reputations as sail-carriers and drivers. The little Adelaide clippers drove through weather that would have caused doubt in the minds of many a master of larger ships, and it was said that they ran their easting down to Cape Leeuwin half submerged by the great seas of the Roaring Forties, so that they looked like masts and sails driving onward before the wind with no deck beneath. Their masters took pride in the fact that they could carry a main topgallant sail when other ships had snugged down to reefed topsails.

Even long after the gold rush days it was not always easy to obtain crews in Australia for home: the long, cold passage of the Horn was not to be welcomed, nor was the prospect of shipping back out of London at fifty shillings a month, and it often happened that a ship's crew would 'run' in Port Adelaide for the pickings to be got in Australia. On such occasions temporary hands, known as voyage runners, had to be found and signed on for the trip round to Port

Augusta, a run of some four hundred miles through Investigator Strait and around the Yorke Peninsula into Spencer Gulf. When these men returned home by other ships, the bereft masters had to find more hands to work their vessels back to England, and many a bushman who had come down country to get blind drunk in 'the Port' was persuaded to sign articles for a trip to London once he had spent himself out. The result was that ships were driven home with the strangest crews ever to sail the seas – bullock drovers, boundary riders, shepherds, all kinds of station hands turned into temporary sailors, some of them men who had been to sea before, but so long ago that they had forgotten all they had learned. However, they found that the knack of handling sail soon came back as the land years dropped away; as for the rest, they found it a gruelling experience and many were the regrets for comfortable shore beds when the constant cry went up for All Hands.

The Orient Line was founded by the firm of James Thompson and Company, who sailed small ships and barques to the West Indies. When James Anderson joined the firm it became known as Anderson, Green and Company, who remained as London operators of the Orient Line, eventually known as the Orient Steam Navigation Company, right through until its absorption by P. & O. in the early Sixties of this century. Their first ship on the Australian run was the *Orient*, 1033 tons, built to take part in the gold rush traffic to Melbourne. She was fitted to take passengers below a poop-deck sixty-one feet in length, but before going into service was requisitioned by the British government for trooping to the Crimea. At the landing at the Alma in September 1854, now named Transport Number 78, she landed the 88th Regiment, the Connaught Rangers, later becoming a hospital ship in support of the operation against Odessa. After hostilities had ceased she was handed back, and on 5 July 1856 sailed out of Plymouth under Captain Lawrence with a full passenger list, to become one of the favourites of the Australian trade.

Five years later, still with Lawrence as master, the *Orient* was to meet misfortune. Leaving Adelaide on 3 November 1861 with 2600 bales of wool plus some copper ore and a number of passengers, she called at the Cape of Good Hope, and left Table Bay on 18 December. During the forenoon of 2 January, a thin trail of smoke was seen coming from her fore hatch. Captain Lawrence at once ordered the lifting of the lower deck hatches, but there appeared to be no fire, or even smoke, in the hold, which indicated that the seat of the trouble was in the 'tween-decks. All hands were turned to the job of breaking out the wool cargo, but once they had reached the third beam aft of the hatchway, they met intense heat and smoke and were driven out of the fore hold. The main hatch was opened up, and another attempt made to break out the cargo from that access, but once again without success, as the crew were driven back.

Opposite the US Coastguard training barque, Eagle, originally the *Horst Wessel* built in 1936.

After this the operation went into reverse: the hatches were battened down hard and every opening closed in an attempt to contain and smother the fire. The carpenter was ordered to bore holes in the deck to admit fire hoses. This work was started in the galley, and he worked gradually forward until he was right over the fire's centre. When that position had been ascertained the fire engine and the condensing engine were brought into play to drench the cargo, and as fast as the water went down it was sucked out again by the pumps in order to preserve the ship's stability and trim. With the deck ports and scupper vents closed, the upper deck itself was kept some inches under water as a safety measure. While the fire-fighting went on, the bosun collected a party of passengers to provision and lower the lifeboats, which were then streamed astern ready for any order to abandon ship. At 5 pm that evening dense smoke was seen to be pouring from the scuttles below the fore chains, and the woodwork was observed to be charring badly; so great was the heat that the glass bull's-eyes had melted. Immediately the order came from the master to plug the scuttles and cut through the deck planking, with the result that smoke and flame burst through like an inferno. Right through the night the crew kept the pumps and fire engine going, and next day, when a Dutch ship came up to stand by the stricken *Orient*, the women passengers were sent across to safety.

After desperate efforts from weary, hard-pressed men the fire was at last smothered. On 5 January the *Orient* arrived at Ascension Island, where a good deal of her cargo was taken out for examination. Temporary repairs were effected, and she made out again to sea, arriving safely in the London River with twelve of her timbers so charred that they were useless for further service, as also was all the main deck planking from the bows to the main hatch. Captain Lawrence had done a fine job of self-salvage, which was highly pleasing to the underwriters; he was presented with a handsome piece of plate worth £100, plus a sum of £800 for himself, his officers and his crew.

By the Seventies, timber as a construction medium was virtually out, replaced by iron, and it was the introduction of iron into shipbuilding that was the primary factor in the developing supremacy of Britain over the United States in the sailing ship trade. Iron killed off the competition, for the Americans' skill lay in their splendid wooden and composite ships, but iron did not kill sail – what finally killed sail was the craze for more and more speed, for bigger ships, for increased luxury in passenger and crew accommodation and fittings, together with a softening-up of the men themselves as steam came into their lives and careers. Blame must go also to the developing structure of the companies, and the emergence of the men known as managers, forerunners of the modern executive. The manager came along to replace the direct contact of the personal owner, the partner who had acted as ship's husband. The ship was now divorced, husbandless, and the spirit of service, of personal involvement, began to wither as the Boards and the Head Office and the agencies grew bigger and more remote.

But though iron was not the killer, it was at first unpopular: it produced strange difficulties. Its effect upon the deviation of the compass caused, in the early days, a number of shipwrecks, strandings and lost directions. As an example, on 19 January 1854 the iron sailing ship *Tayleur*, at 2500 tons the largest merchant ship yet built in Britain, left Liverpool for Melbourne on her maiden voyage, carrying a crew of eighty with possibly more than six hundred passengers – accounts vary as to the size of her passenger list, some giving her a total of 496 emigrants. Driving through a gale of wind under topsails and foretopmast stays'ls the ship, as a result of a false reading given by her magnetic compass, struck the rocks of Lambay Island off the east coast of Ireland. She began to sink fast, and the unfortunate emigrants gave way to panic, losing no time in jumping overboard to what they imagined to be safety, or at any rate comparative safety. The rocks of Lambay, however, proved no kinder than any other rocks, and many were the heads cut open as the frantic men and women were taken by the roaring seas and dashed willy-nilly to their deaths. In spite of the gallantry shown by the ship's surgeon, Dr Cunningham, in his attempts to rescue the passengers from the sea, and in exhorting and encouraging those who managed to reach safety, a very large number of lives were lost – again accounts vary but it is believed that up to 370 souls perished as a result of that simple compass error.

It was not long, of course, before the problem of iron attraction was dealt with, and along came that estimable personage the Compass Adjuster, with his instruments, expertise and attendant tugs to swing the ship point by point through the full 360 degrees, hanging his weights in their proper positions to adjust for deviation at the start of every voyage. Another of iron's drawbacks was its lack of buoyancy as compared with wood: the iron ships tended to run more submerged even than an Adelaide clipper. And without the copper that had sheathed the wooden bottoms, weed and barnacles found a soft option and grew apace, thus cutting speed through the water with trailing hairy crops and shell-upon-shell proliferation. This not only cut speed: in light winds the heavy growth increased the problems of ship-handling.

On the other side of the coin the advantages of iron over wood were solid enough. The iron hulls could withstand an unlimited amount of hard driving and sailing, especially into head seas, and there was much more cargo space available, for in previous years the sheer difficulty of working with wood in big sizes had tended to keep down the tonnage. Iron did away with this restriction, and there was thereafter a steady growth in the size of individual ships – since there was no necessity to increase the crews proportionately, economy of running was well served. It was also a very positive advantage that the iron ships were much less susceptible to the risk of fire.

Iron masts and wire stays caused a sizeable alteration in sail plans: the new ships were loftier than the old, but as the yards became squarer it was found that the fitting of stuns'ls was becoming something of a luxury, and by the early Eighties even a foretopmast stuns'l was regarded as a freak. And the lessons of rigging strains had to be learned all over again with the iron clippers.

The first ship to be built entirely of iron had been launched as far back as 1838, and named, appropriately, *Ironsides*. She came from the Liverpool yard of Jackson, Gordon and Company, and in her appearance was very little different from contemporary wooden vessels. She was very short, with a heavy stern and a lowish bow from which reared a bowsprit of extreme length, her jibboom also being exceptionally long; in contrast to her short hull, her masts appeared sky-high. Although popular with marine artists, who flooded the shop windows with her picture, she could not be said to have been a great success commercially, and iron ships had only a comparatively short life before steel took over.

It was in the Australian trade that the iron passenger ships stood pre-eminent and perfect. These ships, succeeding the great Liverpool clippers and the Blackwall frigates, were in no way inferior, and in the Seventies and Eighties they were a continual draw for the crowds along the London River, the Mersey and the Clyde. In Sydney landsmen took special Sunday excursions to Circular Quay to see the ships lying stately in the splendid harbour of Port Jackson. The iron ships lost London its building trade in the latter half of the century: the shipbuilding centred itself from the Fifties mainly in the Clyde, the Mersey and Aberdeen. The firm of Barclay, Curle produced some fine examples, such as many of the 'Loch' class – *Loch Maree*, *Loch Torridon*, *Loch Carron* among them. Thompson of Glasgow also built 'Lochs' – their masterpiece was *Loch Garry* – as did the firms of Lawrie, Inglis, Henderson, and Connell.

New Zealand

The New Zealand trade was an extension of the run to Australia, and across this extra surge of ocean drove the vessels of Shaw, Savill and Company, mainly ships and barques of 400 to 500 tons that stormed through the Roaring Forties initially with emigrants. One of the best-known of these ships was the *Edwin Fox*, a country-built Indiaman out of Calcutta, launched in 1853, a fine vessel with teak decks, quarter galleries, and coir running gear that, sadly, ended her sea life as a landing stage for the freezing plant at Picton on South Island. In the Sixties, Shaw, Savill began a regular service to New Zealand, sending out fifteen ships a year. Initially the outward passage took between four and five months, but by the next decade the voyage time had been much cut by Shaw, Savill's fast iron ships such as *Crusader*, *Helen Denny* and *Margaret Galbraith*.

The iron ship *Loch Carron*, damaged in a collision with the *Inverkip*.

opposite Loading up at Circular Quay, Sydney, in 1883.

Shaw, Savill had a reputation for a notable lack of luck in regard to collision and fire. One of their most terrible disasters was the fate of the *Cospatrick*, brought under the Shaw, Savill flag in 1873. *Cospatrick* sailed for Auckland, New Zealand, on her second voyage for Shaw, Savill under Captain Elmslie, leaving the London River on 11 September 1874 with a mixed cargo and more than four hundred passengers. On 17 November she was south of the Cape of Good Hope in light north-westerly winds. Henry Macdonald, second mate, below after keeping his watch on deck, was roused out on account of fire. Rushing on deck, he found that fire had broken out in the bosun's store, a place of oakum, tar, paint and rope, and that thick smoke was pouring from the fore peak. While the fire engine was being rigged, the ship's head was put before the wind, to take the smoke and flames forward where they could do no harm; but sadly the ship was allowed to drift off course, and her head came back into the wind, with the result that suffocating smoke clouds were driven aft and the flames licked towards the stern.

Within ninety minutes of the fire's discovery the ship – hull, masts, yards and rigging – was ablaze. Panic gripped the terrified emigrants, who rushed the boats, capsizing the starboard one and causing the longboat to take the flames; the blazing main and mizzen masts fell upon shrieking men and women clustered in the stern. Only two boats got away, with eighty-one souls between them. For two days these boats, with no means of propulsion, remained in the vicinity of the doomed ship; then, charred and smoking still, as black as ink, she sank. After the quarter galleries had blown out, the people in the boats had seen the terrible sight of Captain Elmslie grasping and lifting his wife, who was struggling in his arms, so as to throw her bodily into the water. Then the boats were alone upon the sea, their occupants still in only their night garments and without food or water. Two days later a wind came up, blowing strongly, and they were separated. Thirst plagued the men and women; many died, some of them after becoming mad as the days wore on. A foreign flag ship passed close by the second mate's boat, and was hailed, but she sailed on, taking no notice. The emigrants maintained life by sucking up the blood of the dead before throwing them overboard. Picked up eventually by the ship *British Sceptre*, bound home to Dundee from Calcutta, and landed at St Helena were the final survivors: the second mate and two able seamen, out of almost 480 souls aboard on sailing.

The wool trade from Australia and New Zealand was finally killed, so far as sail was concerned, by the coming of the steamship and the opening of the Suez Canal, which cut the length of the run drastically for the steamers. The frozen meat trade from New Zealand was similarly affected, and the windjammers had to be content with the grain trade from Australia, in which they loaded at Spencer Gulf, and the coal trade from Newcastle, New South Wales, bound for the west coast of America.

6

The Roaring Forties
and Beyond

opposite The deck rolls under the Cape Horn greybeards.

THE Roaring Forties is the seaman's term for that terrible area of storm and continuous wind in the high south latitudes, an area that extends right around the world below Cape Horn and the Cape of Good Hope, down to the southern ice where there is nothing to hinder the great build-up of the racing, roaring westerlies, winds that gust to a hundred knots and more. There is nothing to soften the endless heavy swell that sweeps the Southern Ocean, whilst in actual storm conditions the great Cape Horn greybeards surge and roll, often more than fifty feet from crest to trough.

Below latitude 40 degrees south, the wind has blown without cease since God made the world, blows now, and will continue to blow, though it blows nothing but the ghosts of departed windjammers. That wind blows out of the west all the way around the globe from the Horn to Good Hope, along the waters of the Great Australian Bight and on again by way of New Zealand, back again to Cape Horn. It was these continuously blowing westerlies that made the east-west passage of the Horn such a dreaded one. Very often it took weeks to beat around into the Pacific, the ships having sometimes to go right down to the fringe of the southern ice mass, with its terrible drifting icebergs set in a thousand miles of pack-ice moving in the winds and currents, bergs that could split wood and iron and steel as they ground against the helpless hulls of vessels that became trapped. Endlessly the masters sought the shift of wind that would take them round into calmer water. All too often in those latitudes there would be blinding fog as well, for in spite of the buffeting winds fog could and did form from the impact of the slightly warmer wind upon the icy seas.

It was this passage that ships had to take when bound up the South American coast to Chilean and Peruvian ports for nitrate and guano; or sometimes ships would attempt to make the passage to Australia and New Zealand west about rather than spend time running their easting down below the Cape of Good Hope to the Leeuwin at the western end of the Great Australian Bight. The Horn varied. There were times when the east-west passage could be achieved quickly and if that was done then valuable time could be saved; there was an element of luck about it. But mostly the discomforts of life off the pitch of the Horn were intense: icy cold and wet, with no chance to dry out below in deckhouses or cabins that were, as like as not, washed through by the racing seas, with no hot food if the galley fires had been doused, or drawn in the interest of safety.

Danger to life was always present, and accidents were frequent: men falling from aloft, from icebound yards and stiffened footropes, either to break their backs or limbs on the deck a hundred feet below or to drop into the foaming seas to die in seconds from the desperate cold; men with sea cuts that worked down to the bone, sea boils and sores, bruises, fingers mangled in the sheaves of blocks, or with frostbite; men with disease or serious injury when the master and the

opposite The full-rigger *Joseph Conrad* races in a Cape Horn gale, yards square, with a minimum of canvas set.

steward would turn medicos and, with the unsophisticated aid of the *Ship Captain's Medical Guide* and a stock of primitive cure-alls, bandages and knives effect – sometimes – miraculous recoveries. The master would perhaps perform surgery on the saloon table while the victim held a bottle of rum clenched by the neck between his teeth, and the ship, plunging down the great walls of water into the spume-topped valleys that often spanned a mile from crest to crest, lost her wind and lay helpless and quiet until she lifted again to strain her canvas from the cringles and bring back to men's ears the curious orchestra of a windjammer in heavy weather: the noise of wind and sea and cordage, roars and groans and creaks, and a twanging of backstays each with its own note, high or low. In this, the world's worst area of storm, sudden gusts could rip away the sails or bring down masts in a horrible confusion of tangled rigging and smashed woodwork, and the days preceding arrival off the Horn were always ones of much preparation and overhauling of all rigging, not least the gaskets and ratlines on which men's lives so often depended.

Cape Horn in the nineteenth century was one of the busiest of the shipping routes, for it was around there that all ships for the east coast of North and South America, and for Britain and Europe, came home from Australia and New Zealand. The route knew many tragedies and near tragedies, and many fine ships underwent appalling experiences down in those high south latitudes. In 1859 the Black Ball Line's *Indian Queen*, 1041 tons, sister ship to *Marco Polo*, was carrying forty passengers with a cargo of wool and gold dust from Melbourne to Liverpool; when halfway to Cape Horn, in 60 degrees south, she struck a heavy swell from the west and a gale-force nor'westerly wind. In the middle of the night the passengers and off-watch hands were jerked from their bunks by a shock that ran through the ship, accompanied by sounds of tormented grinding and the crash of broken yards from aloft: the ship had struck an iceberg and was lying broadside to the huge, overhanging mass. All the upper yards and sails were hanging judas – over the side – to starboard, and the foremast was held only by its standing rigging, while the topsail yard lay broken in its slings.

It was a filthy night, filled with rain, and the ship appeared to be sinking; already the master, the first mate and the greater part of the crew had abandoned in the port lifeboat. But the carpenter assured the terrified passengers, mustering on the poop, that the vessel was not making any water. The second mate, by name Leyvret, assisted by the carpenter, Thomas Howard, took charge and set up watches from the passengers and the remainder of the crew, sending the master's son to the wheel. The ship was shovelled clear of the ice that lay thick on the decks, broken but ready to freeze into a solid mass once again. As attempts were made to get some sail on the vessel, the lifeboat was spotted to port; its occupants seemed to be trying to return aboard, but were without oars, and the boat was

opposite Manning the lines to survive the storm.

swept away into thickening fog and was never seen again. Within a short time the *Indian Queen* came clear of the iceberg under her backed cro'jack, coming into easier water on its leeward side.

At daybreak, when all the wreckage was clearly visible, another vast iceberg loomed through the fog, but this was cleared in safety, though only just; and as soon as the ship was in open water the foremast fell clear of its rigging and smashed the longboat to matchwood. When the deck tangle had been cleared away over the side by the use of axes, sweat, and extraordinary courage on the part of the depleted crew, such sail as was possible was rigged and the second mate set a course for Valparaiso, almost four thousand miles away. It took the *Indian Queen* no less than seven days to come clear of all the ice, and she did not in fact do so until she had come up to 54 degrees south. After this, matters slowly improved, and sheers and a new foretopmast were rigged which, with other measures, gave the ship some four to five knots. Assailed by strong winds, *Indian Queen* slowly made her northing, and a month later raised the land south of Valparaiso, being finally towed into the Roads by boats from Her Majesty's Ship *Ganges*.

Californian Gold and the Down Easters
When, in the late forties, the Californian gold rush started, Cape Horn saw more ships than ever before for, as we have seen, many of the prospectors from the eastern and northern states preferred to accept the risk of the sea passage rather than attempt to go overland in those hairy days before the interior had been opened up. So in 1849 no less than 800 ships filled to the gunwales with gold-hungry prospectors made the east-west passage, anything that floated being pressed into service as a passenger-carrier. And the gold fever brought not only the actual prospectors to brave the Horn, not only their hangers-on – saloon keepers, bandits, fan-dancers, prostitutes and other get-rich-quick hopefuls – it also brought men who had realized that wheat, more than gold, could make their fortunes. The fruitful Californian plain proved these people right: the cereal crops of the Pacific coast were superior by far to those of the eastern seaboard. 1862 became the vintage year for the grain harvest, when 145 United States ships with 405 British, German, French, Norwegian and Italian vessels took cargoes from San Francisco and Tacoma, either in the form of bulk wheat or flour in cask.

These were the great days of the Down Easters, the ships built and manned in the New England states and hard driven by tough masters and bullying mates. The storms off Cape Horn led to their emergence in replacement of the clipper ships, whose soft wood led to many sprung seams, resulting in increasingly uneconomic repair bills. The Down Easters, in spite of having shorter masts, simpler construction, no stuns'ls and only half the complement of the clippers,

Nineteenth-century San Franscisco;
to the left are Alcatraz and Angel
Island.

proved excellent sailers, and, being built to carry grain, were more suitable for their heavy cargoes than the clippers had been. Their crews were among the world's toughest, and could be subdued by force alone, hence the savagery of some of the masters and mates. In port the drinking was heavy, especially of the famous 'tarantula juice', a strong beverage consisting of two quarts of spirits, cooked peaches and tobacco-juice diluted – just a little – with water. When these vigorous men were drunk, which was often, they were prone to a remembrance of supposed injustices inflicted afloat, and no man's life was safe until sobriety returned. They had a particular hatred for the professional career seamen – the certificated mates, largely of puritanical New England stock, and often enough bucko bastards too, whirling belaying-pins about the decks with gay disdain for men's feelings, breaking men's jaws with heavy knuckles, swearing fearsomely, and with not an ounce of sympathy in their make-up. Naturally not all were of this breed, and those that were could often be toned down by such fine and humane masters, young men very frequently, as Williams of the *St Paul*, Murphy of *David Brown*, Babcock of *Young America*, and Burgess of *David Crockett*.

Welsh Copper Ore Carriers
Cape Horn was used also by the little ships engaged in the Welsh copper ore trade. The crews of these hardy vessels underwent some of the most gruelling seafaring the world has ever known, running voyage after voyage, year after year, to West Chilean ports. They were mostly barques, but there were several small full-rigged ships as well, plus a few brigs. They were all specially built of British oak, teak,

greenheart and mahogany, and had every possible strengthening device inbuilt to enable them to stand up to the pounding of the rollers and carry safely their bulk cargoes of heavy ore. Yet all too often they were lost; to keep them going at all it was necessary to maintain a continual, watch-on-stop-on manning of the hand pumps that clanked and rattled and sucked the seawater out from the hull to spew back over the side.

An example of these small ore-carriers was the *Ocean Rover* of a mere 548 tons, a composite barque built in 1867 at Sunderland. Her career ended abruptly and surprisingly when, during the war between Chile and Peru in 1879, she was struck by a shell and caught fire. Of others, the barque *Valparaiso* was famous for her fast runs home. The fact that her master was a driver was indicated by the double topgallant backstays with which she was always fitted.

The bigger ships had just as tough a time on that terrible Cape Horn run. The four-masted square-rigger *Falls of Halladale* of the Glasgow Falls Line sailed out of Liverpool on 25 July 1903, making an average passage as far as the Horn. Here, deep in the high south latitudes, she remained for three long weeks off the pitch of the Horn, trying to beat past in the teeth of the gale. After losing nineteen sails and starting a leak, with the pumps' backbreaking motion kept up continuously day and night, a greybeard swept aboard during a blinding snowstorm and smashed the fore-and-aft bridges to splinters. Her master, Captain Thomson, gave up the useless fight, put up his helm, and turned for the Cape of Good Hope to make the passage of the high south latitudes the other way – as many a master had done before him.

The *Valparaiso*, an iron ore carrier famous for her speed.

Antarctic Exploration

Voyages right down into the wastes of the Antarctic continent were a real test of both men and ships. At the start of the nineteenth century a degree of mystery surrounded this grim white land of snow and everlasting ice that covered both land and sea. After the great voyages of Captain Cook in the *Resolution*, it was known that sea encircled the entire world at around latitude 60 south, and that beyond this lay the icebergs and the diabolically dangerous floating pack-ice. That region was still utterly and totally unknown, but a certain assumption could well be made about it – that it was not worth visiting in any case, even if it did contain any land, which was at that time doubtful. However, man's curiosity, his instinct for exploration of the unknown, got the better of him and during the course of the nineteenth century no less than eighteen expeditions sailed for the Antarctic: eight British, one joint British and American, four American, and one each from Russia, France, Germany, Norway and Belgium.

The first expedition set out from Kronstadt in Russia under Favrian Gottlieb von Bellingshausen, an Estonian aristocrat, who sailed with the sloop *Vostok* of 450 tons and the frigate *Mirnyl*, 230 tons, the complement of the two ships totalling some 190 men, all of them hand-picked for an arduous task. The expedition sailed out of Kronstadt in July 1819, calling at Copenhagen and Portsmouth for stores and equipment; then they sailed direct for the Antarctic by way of Tenerife and Rio de Janeiro, anchoring just after Christmas in Queen Maud Bay, where they met the crews of some British sealers. After three days spent surveying the South Georgian coast, Bellingshausen weighed and sailed south, coming soon to the very edge of the unknown, sailing through filthy weather of high winds, stormy seas and terrible snowstorms which brought the visibility right down, making for extremely dangerous sailing in seas containing giant icebergs. Day after day, sighting land at intervals, the expedition went on past wastelands obscured by the foul weather, missing destruction by inches from grounding or collision with floes as they skirted the pack-ice.

Throughout January and February and March of 1820 Bellingshausen sailed his dreadful seas and then, as the southern summer approached its end, turned towards Australia through a hell of storm and wind and driving snow, the whole awful scene overladen with mist and always the chance that they might smash into solid ice. After replenishment in Sydney, he sailed south once again, remaining for more than two months south of the 60th parallel, on a track well south of that taken by Cook. For most of the time *Vostok* was in a leaky condition that meant continual manning of the pumps, and at one stage she had virtually all her sails ripped out, so that the men were ordered to trice up their hammocks in the shrouds so as to make what way they could with bare masts. On another occasion they were trapped in the middle of an icefield on the move, blinded by

opposite Scott's *Terra Nova* photographed through an ice floe.

Expeditions in the Antarctic occasionally sighted land but more often looked out over frozen wasteland day after day – even when looking from the topmost mast.

fog but well able to hear the crunch and pound of the ice, and, somewhere ahead, the sound of breakers. Altogether Bellingshausen's ships were brought, during his two expeditions, no less than six times across the Antarctic Circle, and the land he discovered included the South Shetland group, Peter the First Island, and the South Sandwich Islands.

Whaling and Sealing

From this time on, the whaling and sealing industries started their more southerly operations in a big way: by 1840 there were some four hundred vessels engaged in these trades, and with such dedicated skill and endurance did those hardy, wealth-seeking crews pursue their killing calling that not very long afterwards the area had been hunted almost to extermination. The sealers came initially from Boston, New Haven and Nantucket – some of the hardest men ever to sail the sea, constantly risking their lives in uncharted waters and working under the most dangerous and revolting conditions of blubber and blood. They sailed those savage seas, seas where there was virtually no land between 50 and 70 south, in tiny vessels, seldom more than 300 tons, coppered and caulked and well-found, brig-rigged and carrying small boats topside for working the shallows. Brave men, but brutes: men who worked and killed with the most appalling callousness, blinding the bull seals who kept the cows from wandering off the rocks – blinding them deliberately in one eye so that the killing could take place on the blind side, for if the bulls saw the slaughter of their cows they were apt to up and charge the killers. By 1830 they had slaughtered an estimated five and a half million seals, and the southern fur seal was soon to be practically extinct.

As for whaling, the Basques had been the first fishermen to use the harpoon technique, back in the thirteenth century, and for hundreds of years they had the monopoly of the Atlantic whaling, but by the mid-sixteenth century the Atlantic had been hunted clear of whales, and the industry did not revive until a new species was discovered on the edge of the Arctic. At this point whaling was taken over by the British and Dutch. When this new ground, too, was on the verge of extinction, the Antarctic was starting to be opened up, one explorer after another reporting the enormous whaling potential. So profitable was this vicious trade that in the early days of convict settlement in Australia the convict transports were equipped with whaling gear so that, having landed their human freights, they turned into fishers of whales along the Australian coast, which, together with the waters off Van Diemen's Land and New Zealand, were full of prey.

From the New England states of America the whalers also came to kill, hundreds of them each year from the sealing ports, to fish first of all the Indian Ocean and Brazil breeding grounds and then, as the great mammals were thinned out, marauding farther afield to Japan before dropping down through the parallels to the Southern Ocean's abundance, where they swung out their cedarwood boats in the great game of death and money. And very profitable it was: in 1862 one ship alone, the New Bedford whaler *Corinthian*, brought back a cargo of whale oil and bone that realized a quarter of a million dollars.

The hunting boats, of which usually five were slung from davits with a spare one on chocks between the main and mizzen masts, were so light that two men could lift them, and they could be rowed up to a speed of ten knots by their five oarsmen. The boats' equipment included mast and spritsails, oars, paddles, casks of bread and water, harpoons, lances and whale spades for cutting the blubber, also two tubs in which the harpoon ropes were coiled down, the main tub holding 230 fathoms and the reserve 75 fathoms. So violently did the rope fly out once the unfortunate whale had been embedded with the harpoon that water had to be poured over it to prevent fire from friction. But the whalers did not have it all their own way: whales could strike back, like the bull against the matador, and it is recorded that in 1819 the whaler *Essex* was attacked in the Pacific by an eighty-five-foot sperm whale which used its battering-ram of a head to shatter the ship's timbers and sink her with repeated blows.

The trade was cruel, vicious, cash-orientated to the nth degree, yet it would not be entirely fair to say that the whole intention of its operators was to kill and make profit. The men opened up the Pacific in the first instance, acting as pioneers of the ocean and charting the atolls and islands before moving on to the southern icelands, and both the owners and the masters of the whaling and sealing vessels contributed more to the world at large than mere trading, for the masters were encouraged to be explorers as well. One of these was James Weddell, who penetrated 74 degrees south, like Bellingshausen, farther than Cook had gone. Another was Biscoe, who in 1831 opened up Enderby Land, naming it after his owner.

More Exploration

In the following years more and more of the great southern mass was opened up. John Balleny, who also worked for Enderby, sailed from New Zealand in 1839 in the schooner *Eliza Scott* in company with the cutter *Sabrina*, crossing the Antarctic Circle in 177 degrees east longitude and voyaging westerly where previous explorers had made towards the east, discovering the islands that bear his name. The previous year had seen the dispatch from Britain of a scientific expedition under Captain James Ross. With two old bomb vessels – *Erebus* of 370 tons and *Terror* of 340 tons, ships of great structural strength, if slow, with their bows given additional reinforcement against the pack-ice – Ross pursued his orders to probe the force known as terrestrial magnetism, which was concerning the British Association who had petitioned the government to set up an investigation.

While all this was in course of preparation two other expeditions had already sailed. A French expedition in 1837 comprised the corvettes *L'Astrolabe* and *La Zélée*, under the navigator Dumont d'Urville, who came down from Toulon upon Graham Land intending to follow Weddell's course and reach high latitudes. Frustrated by pack-ice, d'Urville made only minor discoveries after crossing into the Antarctic Circle in December and sailing between South Orkney and South Shetland for some three months before retreating back to Australia. The third of that year's expeditions to set sail consisted of five ships out of Chesapeake Bay under Lieutenant, later Commander, Charles Wilkes. But Wilkes's expedition was poorly equipped and under-financed, and in the early days its members were

in a constant state of bicker. Wilkes pulled the whole thing together and arrived off Tierra del Fuego in March 1839, here dividing his command, sending *Peacock* and *Flying Fish* south-west towards Graham Land and Alexander Land while he himself carried on some survey work. *Peacock* and *Flying Fish*, the latter a cockleshell of less than 100 tons and unstrengthened, managed to force through the ice down to 70 south, which was a real feat of endurance and seamanship. When the season shut down they sailed back to rejoin Wilkes, who made for Sydney to use the southern winter for repair and replenishment of his small fleet, as d'Urville had done.

By this time word had spread in regard to Ross's scientific expedition, though it was known that he could not be in a position to reach the magnetic pole until the following year, 1840. All the same, both Wilkes and d'Urville set sail immediately, the latter leaving Van Diemen's Land in January 1840 and finding an easy passage. When in latitude 66 degrees south, longitude 140 degrees east, he sighted land to the south. He seemed at first to have seen only the long ice barrier that was so typical of the Antarctic coasts, but later he found, beyond the ice-wall, a number of islets, and was able to land and collect rock specimens. He named the coast Adelie Land. Going on westward, he once more sighted the ice barrier a little more to the north, and named it Côte Clarie. Then he turned for the north.

Meanwhile Wilkes had left Sydney back at the end of December. His ships took various tracks but he, aboard *Vincennes*, reached latitude 66 degrees south, longitude 158 degrees east on 16 January, and at this point claimed to have first seen land to the south. He cruised to the west approximately along the latitude of the Antarctic Circle, seeing land most of the way, with comparatively open sea to the north and massed pack-ice to the south. Beyond this ice he claimed to have seen, again and again, what he called high and mountainous land. This was a terrible voyage for hardship, exposure, and danger. At one time *Peacock* lay trapped in the ice, her rudder lost, her anchors dragging, the tempestuous seas smashing her again and again against the ice. The crews of all the ships suffered badly from the freezing cold, from exhaustion, from a lack of proper food – yet they kept going, like all sailormen of the nineteenth century. As in d'Urville's case, Wilkes was blocked by the ice, and managed only to land upon an offshore island near the 100th meridian. This was on 14 February, and a few days later Wilkes set his course northwards for Sydney.

Ross, his own intended route having now been explored, went south along a more easterly track. Sailing in November from Hobart, he reached the Antarctic Circle on 1 January 1840 in longitude 171 east, opposed by heavy masses of pack-ice through which he bravely plunged his specially strengthened heavy ships, forcing them right into the ice and buffeting his way through to the south. It was

a bold stroke that met with great success: for five days Ross pushed on through closely-packed ice floes, and then his ships burst out to the south, into an open sea, and he steered west towards the magnetic pole. On 8 January he discovered the mountain country of Victoria Land.

The Later Cargoes

After 1875, when the control of the passenger and freight traffics had largely passed into the hands of the steamship companies, voyages for the sailing ships tended, curiously perhaps, to become longer. Sail still had the monopoly of certain of the world's routes – for instance, European sailing ships with British coal or general cargoes sailed for New York or Philadelphia where cased petrol might be taken on for the Far East around Cape Horn. They would return via Australia, the American Pacific coast, or Chile, a round-the-world-voyage every time, looking for cargoes where they might be found, the old settled routes and trades fast receding into the past. Heavy goods were loaded for Australia and New Zealand from America – tiles, machinery and cased goods – and the ships came home to Europe with frozen beef or wool, or sometimes took Australian coal up to Chile, loading there with nitrates for Britain and the Continent. Freight bound for the west coast of America was equally mixed, but very often ships had to leave in ballast and then come home with American grain. Higher up the Pacific coast, grain and lumber were loaded at Portland, Seattle, Tacoma, Port Townsend and Vancouver.

Out of British ports, where often coal was loaded at Newcastle, Cardiff and Barry, sailing ships carried on trading to the Chilean coast, to Talcahuano, Valparaiso, Coquimbo, Mejillones, Antofagasta, Caldera, Taltal, Iquique, Caleta, Buena Pisagua – to bring back the nitrates for discharge at Dunkirk, London, Bruges, Antwerp, Rotterdam, Hamburg. From New Caledonia in the Pacific, nickel was loaded at Thio, Canala, Kouaoua and Gomen by ships which brought the ore to Glasgow and Le Havre. Their outward run in ballast was often helped by consignments of European coal for the Nickel Corporation. These Pacific voyages involved the two-way passage of the Horn. The ships had become sailing tramps, voyaging out across most of the world's great seas and oceans, calling at whole gazetteers of rivers and bays, roadsteads and ports, on runs that in many cases lasted for two years and more.

Opposite The Polish *Dar Pomorza* is used for merchant navy training.

7

The Last of the Tall Ships

To all intents and purposes sail in Britain and America had come to an end in any real commercial sense by the end of the first decade of the new century. Nevertheless a number of ships did survive, many of them under new flags. *Cutty Sark*, for instance, passed under Portuguese ownership, sold by Old White Hat Willis in 1895 after she had brought back her biggest-ever wool cargo from Australia. She spent many more years at sea before being bought by Captain Dowman, himself a master in sail, and restored. But from 1910 onwards it was a heart-breaking period for masters whose whole seafaring life had been passed in sail. The crews were inexperienced, and by 1913 there were boys sailing as mates, for by this time all the best men had departed into steam, and no longer could masters sail their ships to the fullest extent, for they knew that the crews would not be able to cope with any emergency.

Fighting Ships under Sail

A number of sailing ships took an active part in the First World War, among them the British windjammer *Pass of Balmaha*, which was captured by the German Navy in the North Sea in the early part of the war, and converted into a commerce raider. Renamed *Seeadler*, and fitted with 1500-horsepower auxiliary engines and an armament of two 4.2-inch guns plus bombs and machine-guns, *Seeadler* masqueraded as the neutral Norwegian *Irma*, sailing on 21 December 1916 with a deck cargo of timber that effectively blocked all entries to the hold other than by secret doors. Provisioned for a three-year voyage, she caused heavy loss to Allied shipping under her commander Count von Luckner, a German naval officer who had sailed as able seaman in sailing ships, including a British one. During her raiding voyage across the Atlantic, *Seeadler* disposed of five French sailing ships, three British, one Italian, and then, sailing around the Horn into the Pacific, sank three American ships before meeting her own end on a Tahitian coral reef.

The English Channel became extremely dangerous to ships, infested as it was by lurking submarines and auxiliary armed cruisers, but Chilean nitrates were much in demand for the manufacture of explosives for shells and had to be brought home. So the sailing ships continued in this trade, crossing the Atlantic from Cape Horn at very great risk.

A number of small sailing ships joined the British Navy's growing fleet of mystery ships, the 'Q' ships that pretended to be unarmed merchantmen but carried Royal Naval crews and concealed guns, and whose job it was to lure the German U-boats within range by appearing to abandon ship, then to run up the White Ensign and open the gunports to blast the surfaced submarine out of the water. One such was the brigantine *Helgoland*, 310 tons gross, built of steel and iron in 1895. She was being overhauled at Liverpool in July 1916 when she was taken over by the British Admiralty and ordered to Falmouth, where she was fitted out as a

left Britain's *Sir Winston Churchill*, built by the Sail Training Association in 1965, for the express purpose of offering young people, between the ages of sixteen and twenty, the opportunity to experience 'training under sail'.

A tall ship torpedoed during the Second World War.

'Q' ship and armed with four 12-pounder guns and one Maxim. Subsequently known by a variety of names – *Helgoland*, *Horley*, *Brig 10* and *Q 17* – she was manned by men of the Auxiliary Patrol at Falmouth, and officered by the Royal Naval Reserve, her crew including six RN gunnery ratings. She sailed out of Falmouth in September, and was immediately in action, coming under fire from an enemy submarine which started shelling her from a range of 2000 yards. Becalmed, it was some while before *Helgoland* could manoeuvre to bring her guns to bear, but once she was able to, she opened with good effect, her fourth round hitting the submarine and forcing it to dive. Then an astonishing incident occurred: a second submarine was sighted aft, a submarine under the power of a sail comparable in size with the mizzen of a drifter – perhaps the only example of a sailing submarine. This vessel also was attacked by the *Helgoland*'s guns, and, laying a smokescreen, dived beneath its cover.

One of the great names among the 'Q' ships under sail was the three-masted steel-built topsail schooner *Mary B. Mitchell*, of 210 tons gross. Requisitioned from the china clay trade whilst lying at Falmouth, she was fitted with three guns and

began her armed career by covering the Western Approaches, remaining at sea for a month on her first cruise, manned largely by officers and men of the Royal Naval Reserve. Another was the three-masted schooner *Prize*, which fought several engagements under Lieutenant Sanders, RNR, who was awarded the Victoria Cross; his crew, which was an outstanding one, included one DSO, two DSCs and many DSMs.

A number of very small sailing craft were similarly involved in war, among them many smacks out of Lowestoft and Brixham, which could carry on with their normal fishing activities and, when attacked, cut their trawls and open up with their concealed armament. One such, the *Telesia* under Skipper W.S. Wharton, RNR, came under torpedo attack on 23 April 1916. Sighting a periscope, Wharton opened fire, sending fifteen rounds across and continuing to fire as the submarine briefly showed her deck. A kill was not confirmed, but the German broke off the engagement. Small in size but big in courage, even the tiny open cobbles out of the Yorkshire fishing ports were used against the submarine menace in protection of coastal shipping plying the North Sea.

Using a US submarine as a U-boat this post-war film re-enacts an attack on a sailing ship.

The Last Great Owner

The last of the great sailing ship owners was Captain Gustav Erikson of Mariehamn in Finland's Aland Islands. Erikson had started his seagoing career as a boy aboard a small barque in the North Sea timber trade. At the age of thirteen he was a sea-cook, then signed as able seaman and later as bosun. At eighteen he was mate of a timber ship, and a year later was given a command. After this he left the timber trade and for five years sailed blue water as a mate in a full-rigged ship, later sailing in command from 1902 to 1913, swallowing the anchor from the Finnish barque *Lochee* of 1753 gross tons and, at the age of forty-one, becoming a shipowner. He bought the German four-masted ship *Renne Rickmers*, renaming her *Aland*. Built by Russell and Company at Port Glasgow in 1887, Erikson's first owned ship became a total loss when, on her maiden voyage under her new flag, she drove on to a reef near New Caledonia.

At the end of the First World War, Erikson, by this time a wealthy man, owned a considerable fleet of sailing ships, and he increased this by informed buying. By the 1930s he owned *Penang*, *Killoran*, *Grace Harwar*, *Winterhude*, all three-masted barques, plus the four-masted barques *Archibald Russell* and *L'Avenir*. To these he

These square riggers in Port Mariehamn were all part of Captain Gustaf Erikson's fleet; from left to right they are: the *Viking, Pommern, Olivebank* and *Pennang*. In the foreground is the bowsprit of the *Herzogin Cecilie*.

added *Lawhill*, *Olivebank*, *Passat*, *Pommern*, *Ponape*, *Viking*, *Herzogin Cecilie* and *Pamir*. Between 1925 and 1935 his fleet consisted of some seventeen ships, half of them built in Germany, half in Britain. His crews were largely Scandinavian with a few adventure-seekers from Britain, America, Germany, Australia and New Zealand, mostly youngsters putting in some sea time before going to navigation schools.

Erikson sailed his ships in the grain trade to Australia, leaving European ports in ballast mainly, though taking the occasional cargo of coal to South Africa, or timber to Melbourne, making the return passage around Cape Horn, the old route of the more spacious seafaring days. As time went on there was less and less in the way of profit; the ships were forced to sail with old and worn canvas and rigging and with small crews many of whom might be amateurs who had paid for their passages. But Gustav Erikson was no ordinary profit-seeker: he was a man who had a deep love for sail and all it had stood for through the centuries, for the way in which it built character and made men. To him this was of much more worth than trading profit, and his ships continued to hold the seas even beyond his death in August 1947 – though from the end of the Second World War the fleet, the last of its kind, was down to six ships, all of which are now gone.

The *Pamir*, spoken by the *Christian Radich*, sets out on what was to be her last voyage.

Last of the big cargo-carriers under sail were the four-masted barques *Passat* and *Pamir*. After 1945 they sailed under the German flag, fitted now with auxiliary engines by Howaldt-Werke at Kiel for use as training ships in addition to their commercial role. They both served the Brazil run, carrying grain, until in 1957 *Pamir*, on passage from the Plate for London, was struck by a hurricane and, with all sail set, was blown on to her beam ends by a tremendous gust of wind. Her bulk grain cargo shifted and she went down with eighty men and cadets, only six being rescued by other ships. She was the last of the old Cape Horners to undertake a commercial voyage. *Passat* is now preserved at Lübeck. Others still remaining as memorials to a great age include the three-masted ship *Balclutha*, ex-*Star of Alaska*, built at Glasgow in 1886 and now enshrined at San Francisco – a ship that as late as 1926 made a two-week passage from San Francisco to Bristol. *Pommern* lies at Mariehamn, and *Viking* at Gothenburg, with the great *Cutty Sark* still proudly lifting her bare poles to the skies over Greenwich.

The building of new sailing ships has not been unknown in the twentieth century, but the number has been sadly small; yet it is curious that in 1911, when it was all nearly over, the world's biggest sailing ship was built at Bordeaux. This was the *France II* already referred to, with a deadweight capacity of 8000 tons. She was water-ballasted and fitted with deep fresh water tanks of 1126 tons capacity. Her main truck was almost 200 feet above the waterline and the total weight of her masts and rigging was a staggering 456 tons. The surface area of her 20 principal sails was 65,000 square feet and her running rigging ran, indeed, for thirty miles. This latterday giant, the dinosaur of sail, carried English coal to New Caledonia via the Cape of Good Hope, Tristan da Cunha and Tasmania, returning with nickel ore around Cape Horn. Sometimes, before returning to Europe, she ran wool and tallow between Australia and New Zealand. On 11 July 1922, when she was lying becalmed off Noumea in New Caledonia, a tidal wave swept up and dashed her violently ashore. She could in fact have been salvaged, but the post-war slump in trade, especially in nickel, made the job not worth the expense.

Running the *France II* close for size was the five-masted barque *Kobenhavn*, launched at Leith in 1921 by Ramage and Company for Danish owners, and destined to serve as a training ship. She was 420 feet in length, with a beam of 49 feet, 3965 tons gross and a full load displacement tonnage of 7000. Of exceptional build, she was fitted with double-bottoms and watertight bulkheads like a steamship, and she carried wireless. Sailed by a crew of sixty-five all told, she disappeared in 1930 between Cape Town and Fremantle, and was believed to have struck ice floating up from the Antarctic whilst running her easting down in the Southern Ocean. Also in 1921 was built *Greta Linnea* from the Stockholm archipelago; and before this, in 1916, the Swedes had produced the three-masted topsail schooner *Ragnar*. 1918 had seen the four-masted schooner *Kaj Hvilsom* built in Denmark, while later, in 1926, came the last three-masted fore-and-aft schooner to be built in Sweden, the *Dagny*. As far back as 1905 the last trading sailing ship to be built for British owners had appeared: the four-masted steel barque *Archibald Russell* which passed under Erikson's flag in 1924. Built by J. Hardie and Company on the Clyde, she remained afloat until she was broken up after the Second World War.

Revival of Sail Training

In recent years there has been some revival: enough young people have discovered an interest in a more romantic age, a tougher and cleaner and slower age, to make worthwhile the provision of sail training ships. In Britain the old style of seafaring has made its comeback with the emergence of the Sail Training

The *Eagle* visits Europe and the Caribbean annually carrying cadets of the US Coastguard on training cruises.

Association's three-masted topsail schooners *Malcolm Miller* and *Sir Winston Churchill*, each of 300 tons Thames measurement. The aim is not specifically to produce professional seamen but to give youth its chance to live and work together in conditions of danger and discomfort, to teach young men and women self-reliance and confidence in themselves and their fellows in moments of crisis, to teach leadership and, above all, to build the foundations of character. It is a tacit acceptance of the tremendous value of the great days of sail. These vessels were built in 1965 and 1967 respectively, the one by Richard Dunston at Hessle in Yorkshire and the other by John Lewis of Aberdeen; they are 135 feet in length, with a 25-foot beam and a draft of 16 feet. They carry a gaff and topsails on the fore and main masts, and Bermudian rig on the mizzen, and there is a square sail on the foremast. The truck of the mainmast rises 112 feet above the waterline. There are two auxiliary diesel engines each of 135 horsepower. The vessels are designed to carry thirty-nine trainees plus a permanent crew under an experienced master and chief officer, and each batch of trainees spends a little under a fortnight aboard, the cruises taking them to many Continental as well as British ports.

In America too there is a strong revival of interest in sail, and it is being suggested by naval architects that the soaring costs of fuel oil may once again make sail a viable commercial proposition. In the meantime young Americans are getting their hands in aboard the sailing ships of the Harry Lundeburg School of Seamanship at Piney Point, Maryland, a joint venture of the International Seafarers' Union and private shipping lines. The United States is one of twenty nations of the world that still believe in the enormous value of square-riggers for the training of naval cadets. Midshipmen of the US Coast Guard Academy at New London, Connecticut, sail aboard the steel barque *Eagle*, carrying twenty-two sails, towards the Atlantic and the Caribbean, while the town of Camden, Maine, prides itself on being today the windjammer capital of the world, where all kinds of sailing vessels are reconstructed. On Chesapeake Bay the last of the sailing oyster fleets still works from November through March – just around thirty wooden bugeyes, skipjacks and schooners left, of the 300-odd that used to race their catches to Baltimore and Annapolis. Still at sea is the old *Chester Peake*, built for the oyster trade in 1915 and restored by a brewing company in the late Sixties.

Of the countries that still maintain sail training ships for their naval services, Russia is believed to stand head and shoulders above the others, but no details are available. It is perhaps significant that what is rapidly becoming the world's most powerful navy still adheres to the old ideas. Among the others are the Argentine, with their full-rigged steel-built *Libertad* of 3765 tons gross, fitted with engines but carrying twenty-seven sails; 338 feet long with a beam of 41 feet and a draft of just under 22 feet, she carries a total complement of 351 souls, including forty-nine deck and thirty-nine engine-room cadets. The Chilean Navy sails the *Esmeralda*, a

opposite above Boys training under sail are stowing the sails aboard the Danish *Georg Stage*; *opposite below* Often as many as four sail-training cadets were needed to hold the wheel which was geared to the rudder by hand aboard the 3000 ton *Herzogin Cecilie*.

overleaf The Chilean training ship, *Esmeralda*.

four-masted steel topsail schooner of 3500 tons displacement and a sail area of 30,000 square feet to take her 370-foot length through the oceans. West Germany trains her cadets aboard the steel barque *Gorch Fock 11*, built in 1958 by Bloehm and Voss in Hamburg. She has a displacement of 1760 tons and an overall length of 293 feet, and carries twenty-three sails, including in her complement no less than two hundred officer and petty officer cadets.

So these ships among others, intended to train for war rather than to trade in peace, are the last of that long line that started with the Romans and their oar-steered open galleys and reached its finest heights in the wonderful years of the nineteenth century, when the great ships stormed east to China and south to Australia, and all around the world below Cape Horn. The men who sailed them, the iron men, the greatest sailors the world has ever known, were a breed that will never, surely, be seen again. They are well worthy of remembrance.

opposite The *Christian Radich* and the *Stratfraad Lehmkuhl*, Norway's entrants in the Tall Ships Race at Plymouth, 30 July 1970; *below* the *Georg Stage*.

Bibliography

Albion, R. G. *Square Riggers on Schedule*, Princeton University Press, 1938; Oxford University Press, 1938.

Cameron, I. *Antarctica, The Last Continent*, Cassell & Co. Ltd., 1974.

Campbell, G. *China Tea Clippers*, Adlard Coles, 1974.

Carrothers, W.A. *Emigration from the British Isles*, Frank Cass & Co. Ltd., 1965; P.S. King, 1929.

Chatterton, E.K. *Q Ships and Their Story*, Sidgwick & Jackson, 1923.

Chandler, G. *Liverpool Shipping*, Phoenix House Publications, 1960.

Clark, Capt. A.H. *The Clipper Ship Era*, 7 C's Press, 1970, 1910.

Coleman, T. *Passage to America*, Hutchinson, 1972.

Culver, H.B. *The Book of Old Ships*, Garden City Publishing Co. Inc., 1935.

Derby, W.L.A. *The Tall Ships Pass*, Jonathan Cape Ltd., 1937; reprinted, David and Charles, 1970.

Greenhill, B. *The Great Migration*, National Maritime Museum and HMSO, 1968.

Guillet, E.C. *The Great Migration*, University of Toronto Press, 1963; Thomas Nelson & Sons Ltd., 1937.

Hyde, F.E. *Liverpool And The Mersey, The Development of A Port 1700–1970*, David & Charles Ltd., 1971.

Jones, C.B.C. *Pioneer Shipowners*, Liverpool Journal of Commerce and Shipping Telegraph, Charles Birchall & Sons Ltd., 1935.

Kennedy, J.F. *A Nation of Immigrants*, Hamish Hamilton, 1964.

Knight, F. *The Clipper Ship*, Collins Sons & Co. Ltd., 1973.

Lubbock, B. *The Opium Clippers*, Brown, Son & Ferguson, 1933.

– *The Down Easters*, Brown, Son & Ferguson, 1929.

– *The Last of The Windjammers*, Brown, Son & Ferguson, 1927.

– *The Colonial Clippers*, Brown, Son & Ferguson, 1924.

– *The China Clippers*, Brown, Son & Ferguson, 1919.

– *Round the Horn before The Mast*, John Murray Ltd., 1902.

Lubbock, B. and Spurling, J. *Sail*, Grosset & Dunlap, 1972, 1925.

MacGregor, D.R. *Fast Sailing Ships 1775–1875*, Nautical Publishing Co. Ltd., 1973.

– *The Tea Clippers*, Conway Maritime Press Ltd., 1972.

– *The China Bird*, Chatto & Windus Ltd., 1961.

Randier, J. *Men And Ships around Cape Horn*, Arthur Barker, 1968.

Scott, Capt. R.F. *The Voyage of The Discovery*, John Murray, 1929.

Svensson, S. *Sails through The Centuries*, Macmillan Publishers Inc., 1965.

Acknowledgements

The author wishes to express his thanks to: Messrs. Brown, Son & Fergusson for their kind permission to quote on page 88 from *The Colonial Clippers* by Basil Lubbock; the staff of the National Maritime Museum, Greenwich, for assistance in research reading; and Mr R. Burrell, ALA Reference Librarian of the City of Southampton for his very valuable help in the selection of reading matter.

The author and publishers would also like to thank Ambrose Greenway and Popperfoto for supplying most of the illustrations in this book and the following who kindly supplied additional material:

Roger Bonnet, *89* (above)
British Museum (Natural History), *73*
Camera Press, *25*, *89* (below)
Mary Evans Picture Library, *64–5*
National Maritime Museum, Greenwich, 10, *26–7*, *45*, *54*, *71*, *108*, *134–5*
Radio Times Hulton Picture Library, 49
Science Museum, London, 14

Numerals in italics indicate colour illustrations

Picture research by Judith Aspinall

Index